ENDORSEMENT

Adversity Comes and Adversity Goes

If you are seeking a book that will impart truth from the Word of God and fuel your faith, then this book is a must have! Just as it has done for me, Adversity Comes and Adversity Goes will inspire you with its content and ignite your faith with its practicality. The words come alive on every page, renewing and reinvigorating our trust in God and His Word.

I know you will be inspired as you read and practice the infallible truths Brenda outlines in this "easy to read" book. This is a timeless piece of work!

Brenda Oglesby is an anointed, passionate and incredibly talented woman of God. Her passion and love resonate throughout the pages of her latest literary gift, Adversity Comes and Adversity Goes. As you delve into each page, I know you will be blessed!

Dr. Leola S. Steward
Co- Pastor
Restoring Hope International Fellowship Church
Webster, Texas

Adversity Comes
and
Adversity Goes

Walking Out Your Blessing

BRENDA OGLESBY

WESTBOW°
PRESS
A DIVISION OF THOMAS NELSON
& ZONDERVAN

Scripture quotations taken from the Holy Bible, New Living Translation, copyright 1996, 2004. Used by permission of Tyndale House Publishers, Inc., Wheaton, Illinois 60189. All rights reserved.

Scripture taken from the King James Version of the Bible.

Scripture taken from the Amplified Bible, Copyright © 1954, 1958, 1962, 1964, 1965, 1987 by The Lockman Foundation. Used by permission.

WestBow Press books may be ordered through booksellers or by contacting:

WestBow Press
A Division of Thomas Nelson & Zondervan
1663 Liberty Drive
Bloomington, IN 47403
www.westbowpress.com
1 (866) 928-1240

ISBN: 978-1-4908-7072-4 (sc)

Library of Congress Control Number: 2015902786

Print information available on the last page.

WestBow Press rev. date: 04/07/2015

DEDICATION

I dedicate this book to my Heavenly Father who is the only Highest God. Blessing, Honor & Praise go to my Father who sits on the throne. I thank you Lord for giving me this book.

CONTENTS

CHAPTER ONE

Walk it Out

This is Your Chance!

When you have a word from the Lord, you have to walk it out. God spoke to you for a reason. He gave you the Word so that you could move into action. You can't stand still and do nothing. You have to walk in the blessing of the Lord. He did not give you His Word for you to sit on it. You must act with confidence on the Word that God speaks to you.

Why haven't you acted on the word that God has spoken to you? I'll tell you why, unbelief. Unbelief means you simply do not believe, and it can manifest in different ways. Maybe, someone has convinced you that the word you received is not true, or perhaps fear has caused you not take action. You may lack the knowledge of what to do, you may be discouraged or you may lack confidence in your abilities. All of these are things can contribute to unbelief.

God has given us plenty of promises in the Bible. I am referring to these promises when I say that God has given you a word. In the Bible, God has promised that His people will be financially blessed and be in excellent health. His word promises salvation and deliverance. God also promised protection, blessings, guidance and much more for believers and their families. All these promises are in the Bible. Take time to read the scriptures and reflect on what God has promised to you.

What promises has God given to you through visions or dreams? Now, think on how you are going to do your part in making those promises come to pass. Oh yes, we have to do our part, but God works out the plan and gives us the victory. *"We can make our plans, but the Lord determines ours steps," (Proverb 16:9, NLT).* God will direct you in the plan as you work it out. You have to start working toward achieving the promise that God has given to you; then, God will intervene and give you the victory. Only then, will you experience the fullness of God's blessings. Your action is evidence of your faith, and it is faith that pleases God. **Right now!** You have to believe the word of God **AND** act on that word. **You can experience all the blessings that are stated in the Bible.** God is still in the blessing business. The book of Hebrews 13:8 says that, *"Jesus Christ is the same yesterday, today and forever."* What God did long ago, He is still doing today and much more. Because of His grace, God will do it for you. It does not matter what is going on in your life, you just have to believe.

Jesus told his disciples *"At that time you won't need to ask me for anything. The truth is you can go directly to the Father and ask him, and he will grant your request because you use my name." (John 16:23, NLT).* Some of you think that God will not bless you because you are living in sin. But God will bless you when you repent and turn from those fruitless ways. God is a Redeemer. So if you are living in sin, you can still be blessed. Ask God for forgiveness and make a complete departure from that sin. You can do that right now; so, that you can start walking in obedience to receive the blessing of the Lord. 1 John 1:9 says, *"But if we confess our sins to him, he is faithful and just to forgive us and to cleanse us from every wrong."* God will forgive you and all you have done. You are immediately made right with God, and at that point you can move forward into His blessings. God forgets all the wrong you have done. *"I, yes, I alone am the one who blots out your sins for my own sake and will never think of them again." (Isaiah 43:25 NLT)*

Now, let me give you six points that will help you move forward into God's blessing; the promises that he made to you about your life.

1. Believe the Word of God, because God keeps his Promises.

The book of Ephesians says, *"How we praise God, the Father of our Lord Jesus Christ, who has blessed us with every spiritual blessing in the heavenly realms because we belong to Christ," (Ephesians 1:3 NLT)*. God has already blessed you, and all of our blessings are located in the spirit realm. The blessings that God already has for you can be accessed by believing the word of God and what God has promised to do in your life. If God has not yet told you what He will do for you, just spend some time with him. He will reveal his plan to you. When you have a word from God, you can believe that it will come true. No matter how the situation looks, you have to say, "I believe God." Romans 3:3 says, *"True some of them were unfaithful, but just because they broke their promises does that mean that God will break his promises?"* God keeps all of his promises. No matter how long it takes, the word of the Lord will come true. God has called his people to believe in the promises he has made to them. Your job is to believe that He will bless you. It is God's job to give you the blessing.

The word says that God will hasten to his word to perform it. God has not called you to worry or try to figure out how the promises he made to you will come to pass, but he has called you to trust and believe that he will do it for you. God called Abraham a righteous man, because he believed the word of the Lord. *"And Abram believed the Lord, and the Lord declared him righteous because of his faith" (Genesis 15:6, NLT)*. Abraham, in his heart, believed and trusted what God told him. This is how you must believe. **You must have faith to believe God's word and trust that He is able to carry it through.** *"Now glory be to God! By his mighty power at work within us, he is able to accomplish infinitely more than we would ever dare to ask or hope" (Ephesians 3:20, NLT)*.

God is able to do more than our minds can imagine. God is able to do more than we can hope for. God is able to do more than we can ask for. He is mighty, and He does mighty works for his children.

Let us be like Abraham and wait patiently, without doubting; and we, too, will receive the promises of the Lord. God does not break his promises. God is a covenant-keeping God, and God does not forget the promises that He made to you in the Bible. *"God is not a man, that he should lie. He is not a human, that he should change his mind. Has he ever spoken and failed to act? Has he ever promised and not carried it through?"(Numbers 23:19 NLT).* God does not lie. You might forget or change your mind, because the promises may seem long in coming. But God never forgets, and He never changes his mind. *"God also bound himself with an oath, so that those who received the promise could be perfectly sure that he would never change his mind" (Hebrews 6:17 NLT).* God has bound himself with an oath that He will bless us, and He will. Therefore, in the right season, the blessing that you are looking for will come. Remember, what Solomon said *"There is a time for everything a season for every activity under heaven" (Ecclesiastes 3:1 NLT).* Your season will come, and it will come soon. Appreciate God's perfect timing. Trust and believe God. I believe God, and you should also.

Don't be like the Israelites. They did not believe the word of the Lord; and, they could not move forward into the promises God had for them. The end results were bad for them. A generation of Israelites died in the wildness because of unbelief. They did not trust God. They did not believe that God would keep his promise to deliver and bless them. They were disobedient, because of their unbelief. And their lack of belief in God stopped them from entering into the promises of God. That is why you must believe God, so that you can enter into the promises of God. The book of Hebrews chapter 3, says don't be like the Israelites that wandered forty years in the wilderness. They did not enter into God's rest (the Promised Land; the promises of God) because of unbelief. So they died in the wilderness; because, they did not trust the Lord. The scripture says, *"For if we are faithful to the end, trusting God just as firmly as when we first believed, we will share in all that belongs to Christ (Hebrews 3:14 NLT)".* We have to trust God as we did when we first believed and received salvation. If we trust and believe him, then what belongs to Christ belongs to us. When we received Christ as our Savior we belonged to him and we inherited God's blessing because of what Christ did on the cross. Now that we belong to Christ we receive his inheritance. Ephesians 3: 6 says, *"The Gentiles have an equal share with the Jews in all the riches inherited by God's children, both groups have believed the Good News, and both are part of the same body and enjoy together the promise of blessing through Christ Jesus"*. Nothing is left out. God is talking about all of his blessings that we can receive because we belong to him and we believe in his promise. All of Christ blessings belong to us *"And my blessing are for the Gentiles, too, when they commit themselves to the Lord" (Isaiah 56:3 NLT)*. Therefore, since we are committed to God, we will be blessed. It is not by our own merit; but, because Christ died on the cross so that we could have a better life. This better life that is offered to us now includes all of the precious promises that God has made to us in the Bible. We have a covenant promise from God that he would bless us and we can receive his best. God's promise of blessing is still here today and only the ones that believe will enter into God's rest which is God's place of blessing. Today, believe the Word of God that you may enter into his blessing for your life. God's word is just and true and it will happen just like He promised. And the scripture says, *"So take courage! For I believe God. It will be just as he said" (Acts 27:25, NLT)*.

2.   Watch who you surround yourself with.

Are the people you surround yourself with full of faith, or are they negative? Separate yourself from unbelievers.

I am not talking about people who do not believe in Christ, but people who do not believe in the promises of God. People who do not believe in the promises of God will sometimes make you negative therefore missing the promises of God. Sometimes God can change their hearts about his promises through your positive attitude, or even by the way you live making them believers of the promises. When that happens that is good for both parties. But, if they heart stay harden against God's word and you do not separate yourself from them then you will end up like them, having nothing.

Is there anything too hard for God? All things are possible with him. Negative people will get you off focus and stop you from moving into God's promises because of their lack of faith. I am not only talking about your enemies; I am talking about your family and friends. Your family and friends can lead you astray; if, they don't believe in your vision or dream. Don't be lead by an unbeliever, because the scripture says in Luke 6:39 *"What good is it for one blind person to lead another. The first one will fall into a ditch and pull the other down also."* So separate yourself from unbelievers. They can lead you to your downfall. Surround yourself with people of faith. 2 Corinthians 6:14 says, *"Don't team up with those who are unbelievers. How can goodness be a partner with wickedness? How can light live with darkness?"* Why would you want to team up with an unbeliever? People that do not believe the word of God are dead to it. Numbers 32:9-12, talks about the Israelites how they did not believe the good report of Joshua and Caleb, concerning The Promise Land. Instead, they believed the bad report from the other scouts that said they could not conquer the land because of the giants that lived there. As a result, the Israelites failed to move into their blessing by believing the wrong people. This prevented them from receiving the blessing that God had for them. Do not repeat what the Israelites did; surround yourself with people that believe that God can bless them right now, here on earth. God has eternal blessings for us, but He also has blessings for us now. Follow God's word with all you heart and you will receive His blessings. **So again, surround yourself with people that believe like you, having faith in God that He will bless you right NOW.**

3. Blessing sometimes comes with trials and tribulation:

There are times when your blessings will come with trials and tribulation, but you will still be blessed. David was blessed, but he had problems with his children. Solomon was blessed, but in the end he lost part of his kingdom. Jacob was blessed by the Lord, and he almost lost his family in a famine. God has so much love and grace and mercy toward us that he delivers us from all of our troubles. *"The Lord hears his people when they call to him for help. He rescues them from all their troubles (Psalm 34:17, NLT)"*. By God's grace you are still blessed when you go through trials and tribulations. And your trials will not last always. *Just* remember what Paul told the Corinthians, *"that is why we never give up. Though our bodies are dying, our spirit is being renewed every day. For our present troubles are quite small and won't last very long. Yet they produce for us and immeasurably great glory that will last forever. So we don't look at the troubles we can see right now, rather, we look forward to what we have not yet seen. For the troubles we see will soon be over, but the joys to come will last forever (2 Corinthians 4:16-18, NLT).* **We don't look at our conditions or present situation. We look to God.** He is the one that will give us victory if we don't give up, lose faith and quit. Believe! Our present trouble is only temporary.

4. When God blesses you, you need to be a blessing to someone else.

God told Abraham in the book of Genesis, *"I will cause you to become the father of a great nation. I will bless you and make you famous, and I will make you a blessing to others. I will bless those who bless you and curse those who curse you. All the families of the earth will be blessed through you"* *(Genesis 12:2-3, NLT).* **The same anointing of blessing that was on Abraham is on us today.** When God blesses us, it is our duty to bless others. God wants his glory spread through-out the world, and

He uses us to do that. God planned this long ago. He told this plan to the prophet Isaiah. *"And my blessing are for Gentiles, too when they commit themselves to the Lord" (Isaiah 56:3, NLT).* Therefore, God's blessings are for everyone who serves him. Paul said, *"But when the right time came, God sent his Son, born of a woman subject to the law. God sent him to buy freedom for us who were slaves to the law, so that he could adopt us as his very own children. And because you Gentiles have become his children, God has sent the spirit of his Son into your hearts and now you become his children. God has sent the Spirit of his son into your hearts, and now you can call God your dear Father, now you are no longer a slave but God's own child. And since you are his child everything he has belongs to you" (Galatians 4:4-7, NLT).* Since we are God's children, everything that belongs to his Son Jesus belongs to us. We can receive the blessing of the Lord for our lives, now and when we do; God wants us to be a blessing to someone else. This is how God's goodness is spread throughout the nations.

5. Be diligent; don't let anything stop you from moving into God promises.

Don't let the devil, people, money, or situations stop you from moving forward. You should move forward even if you have to take small steps of faith. God is looking to see if you believe him. When you start walking in what God has called you to do, the provision you need for your vision or dream will manifest. Faith without works is dead. The book of James says, *"So you see it isn't enough just to have faith. Faith that doesn't show itself by good deeds is no faith at all, it is dead and useless" (James 2:17, NLT).* So, what do you have? Do you have dead faith or faith that is in action? You need to have faith that is in action. Faith that is in action is faith that is moving forward toward the vision or dream that God has given you. You have to work toward your vision or dream to make it happen.

Yes, you can believe that God will make your dreams or vision come true. God is not a God that lies. God will do all He says He will do. I don't care how the situation looks. If God has told you that He will do something for you; yes, believe it. But you must take it a step further with your works. You have to put your faith into action. You have to work on that dream or vision God has given you. If God says that you will be a pilot, then go to flight school. That is working toward your dream or vision. Do you understand what I mean? Let me give you another example. God has promised you a large, beautiful, new home, and you just sit there waiting for the home to come to you. And why don't you take action to move into your new home? Maybe, it's because no one in your family has ever owned a house; or because you don't have any money; or you do not have good enough credit to buy a house. This is looking at self and not at God. So you say, "I am waiting on God to send me the blessing He promised me, while doing nothing towards obtaining the dream or vision. Then you justify your lack of effort toward your dream or vision by your circumstances and present condition, because you are not looking to the Lord. **God will manifest the blessing in spite of any condition or situation.** Paul says in 2 Corinthians 4: 17 that, *"For our present troubles are quite small and won't last very long"* We do not look at our conditions or our present situation. We look to God. He is the one that will give us victory, when we don't lose faith and give up. Our present condition and circumstance are subject to change at any time. That is why we look to the Father for our blessing and not at what we can do. It is God who brings our blessings to pass, not us, or people, or money, but God. Mark 11:22 says *"Have faith in God"*. Get up and go look for a house. Find a Realtor. Go to the bank and get information about a mortgage. Get your credit in order. This is faith in action. Soon you will be in your new home, because God will open doors for you, just because you put your faith into action. This is what the lepers did in the book of 2 Kings Chapter Seven. They walked in faith toward the blessings of the Lord. Not only did they get blessed, they were also a blessing to everyone else. The lepers said "Why sit here and die? We can't go back. We will die in there, too." So they got up and went forward. And when they did, God made the Aramean army hear the footsteps of a large army coming to attack them. When the lepers arrived in the Aramean camp, the whole army had fled leaving all their possessions. What a miracle and a blessing! They were able to plunder the entire camp and enter into God's rest because of their faith in action. So walk in faith believing that God will answer; no matter what the circumstance.

Believe in your dream or vision and don't let anything or anyone stop you from obtaining it. **Don't be like a lot of people who say they are waiting on God.** Well, let me tell you today; God is waiting on you. He is waiting for you to do something in faith. Your provision only comes after you start doing something in faith. When you start walking in faith all that you have been looking for: finances, help from friends and open doors will start happening for you. God will open doors for you when you show him that you believe. God knows that you believe by your actions.

6. Be Patient.

Don't become impatient if your blessing doesn't come when you expect it to come. Sometimes you have to wait on God's promise, but be assured that it will surely come. God told Habakkuk, "*write the vision and make it plain upon tables that he may run that readeth it. For the vision is yet for an appointed time, but at the end it shall speak, and not lie; though it tarry, wait for it; because it will surely come, it will not tarry.*" *(Habakkuk 2:2-3, KJV)*. Your promise will surely come, but there are times when you have to wait. God is getting you and maybe others ready to receive the blessing during the waiting period. So be patient and don't be discouraged. Everything will work out in God's perfect timing. And you will receive what God has promised you.

Solomon says in the book of Ecclesiastes 3:1 that, *"There is a time for everything, a season for every activity under the heaven"*. Remember, your time will come, and it will come when you least expect it. James says that *"God blesses the people who patiently endure testing. Afterward they will receive the crown of life that God has promised to those who love him" (James 1:12, NLT)*. And that crown of life is all the blessings of healing, prosperity, protection, joy, peace, and love. Everything that is perfect in heaven will be yours when you refuse to doubt and believe God instead. Then you will receive God's very best for your life. **God is never late.** Hallelujah! God is not a liar, and He keeps all his promises. If God told you that He will do something for you and you have been waiting for a long time, don't give up, because it will surely come to pass. Luke *18:1(amp)* says *"that they ought always to pray and not to turn coward faint, lose heart and give up"*. If you do not give up on God, He will not give up on you and you will receive the victory. Be like Paul and continue to run your race. **Never give up.** Paul says, *"No, dear brothers and sisters, I am still not all I should be, but I am focusing all my energies on this one thing. Forgetting the past and looking forward to what lies ahead. I strain to reach the end of the race and receive the prize for which God, through Christ Jesus, is calling us up to heaven" (Philippians 3:13-14, NLT)*. Keep running the race. Never give up. **Keep your eyes on the Lord and not your problem.** Believe God. For God will not fail you. He will not leave you. He will surely deliver on his promises in **your** appointed season.

Chapter Two

What's Preventing You from Moving into the Promises?

Walk out your Blessing

Once you become aware of what is preventing you from moving into your blessing, you must deal with that problem. Do not allow the problem to hinder you. Know that there will be trials, tribulations and circumstances that might stop you from moving forward, slow you down or make you want to quit. This happens to everyone that is walking in the plan of God. However, when you don't give into these circumstances you can move into God's blessings. What is your circumstance that is keeping you from moving forward? Are you discouraged, angry, worried, depressed, impatient, weary or do you have a defeat attitude. Again, you must recognize what circumstances are hindering you, so that you can make corrections and move forward into God's plans. This chapter will help you identify your problem and give you insight on what to do.

Your circumstances can bring defeat.

Your circumstances can bring defeat when you allow the circumstances to create negative emotions that control your mind. Following are some of the negative emotions that can prevent you from moving forward.

Discouragement will make you want to stop or even quit, because it can make you lose hope and doubt God's word. If you do not deal with discouragement, it will keep you from moving forward. Turn your discouragement into an opportunity to do good for the Lord. You should always identify what you are discouraged about. **Then think about how great God is and how He will deliver you.** Closely evaluate your circumstances and ask God for the solution. Once God gives you the answer stay focused on the answer. Do not focus on your circumstances. Your answer is your opportunity to do good for the Lord and for you to receive a blessing. You should pray when you feel discouraged like Hannah did in 1 Samuel 1:10-18. Once Hannah overcame her discouragement and sadness, she received the blessing of the Lord. Don't become discouraged, because God has a plan for your life.

Anger can result from trails, tribulations and circumstances and cause you to sin. Anger is an emotion that you can become controlled by because of your problems. Your focus should not be on your problem, but God. The scripture says in Psalms 103:8, *"That you should be slow to get angry and full of unfailing love"*. When your anger controls you; you do not operate in love. Ungodly speech comes out your mouth and makes your curse God's creation. God said, *"cursed be their fierce (Genesis 49:7, NLT)"*. You must operated in love at all time so that you will not be cursed by God and lose your blessing.

Worrying will steal your joy. Again, you are focused on the problem and not God. The scripture says, *"Give all your worries and cares to God, for He cares about what happens to you" (1 Peter 5; 7, NLT)*. God cares for you and you must turn all of your worries over to Him. Paul tells the Philippians, *"Always be full of joy in the Lord. I say it again rejoice! Don't worry about anything instead pray about everything" (Philippians 4:4-6, NLT)*. Why did Paul tell the Philippians not to worry? Paul's desire was for the people to experience God's peace. We too will experience God's peace when we give all our worries to Him.

Depression can be brought on by trials. You feel sorry for yourself and think that you cannot do any better. You often ask yourself why am I experiencing these trials. You feel as though you are the only one going through trials. However, Peter says, *"Remember that your Christian brothers and sisters all over the world are going through the same kind of suffering you are" (1Peter 5:9, NLT)*. **You are not alone in your trials and tribulations.** *"God rains on the just and the unjust. If you share in God's glory you must share in his suffering" (Romans 8:17, NLT)*. Being focused on your circumstances and not looking ahead to the blessing can stop you from moving forward. Don't let your circumstances bring defeat in your life. You have to recognize your depression and cast down that stronghold and move forward.

Impatience happens when the blessing is delayed according to when we think it should happen. God will come at a set time and He will not be late. Solomon said, *"There is a set time for everything a season for every activity under heaven" (Ecclesiastes 3:1, NLT)*. Your set time will come. Keep on waiting for God to move on your behalf. God will always renew your strength. So, wait on the Lord. *"Wait on the Lord, be of good courage, and he shall strengthen thine heart, wait, I say, wait on the Lord" (Psalms 27:14, KJV)*.

Weariness comes when you get frustrated with waiting. You say to God I am tired of waiting. God do it now. The scripture says, *"Don't grow weary in well doing because you will reap if you faint not" (Galatians 5:7 NLT)*.

Handle your circumstances with joy.

When negative circumstances occur, you must face every obstacle with joy. The scripture says, *"Whenever troubles come your way, let it be an opportunity for joy" (James 1:2 NLT)*. The trials that come your way will make you strong, give you patience, and move you into God's plans for your life. As a Christian, you work through your obstacles and let God solve your problems. As you keep your eyes on Jesus you are guaranteed victory. *"You will keep in perfect peace all who trust in you, whose thoughts are fixed on you" (Isaiah 26:3, NLT)*.

You can also profit from your problems. *"And we know that God causes everything to work together for the good of those who love God and are called according to his purpose for them" (Romans 8:28 NLT).* God can work out every bad situation; and He can take a bad situation and turn it into good so that He will get all the glory. What the devil meant to harm and hurt you with, God can turn it around and make it be a blessing to you. **So never let trials, tribulation or circumstances stop you from doing what the Lord says.**

"In everything give thanks for this is the will of God in Christ Jesus concerning you" (1Thessalonians 5:18 NLT). You should give God thanks for every small and large problem in your life. We should believe and know in our hearts that God can handle any, and all of our problems.

Know that your circumstances will not last long.

Trials, tribulations and circumstances are all the same. Even though they may seem so overwhelming at times, they can actually help you to become stronger. When you go through problems you build your faith, you gain more patience, and you grow closer to God. If you trust God, He will use your problems for your benefit. Paul says in 2 Corinthians 4:17-18 that, *"For our present troubles are quite small and won't last very long. Yet they produce for us an immeasurably great glory that will last forever! So we don't look at the troubles we can see right now, rather we look forward to what we have not yet seen. For the troubles we see will soon be over, but the joys to come will last forever".* **The circumstances that you are going through right now will not last very long; but, while you are going through they will build in you greater and stronger character that God will be able to use for his glory.** So, you must not get sidetracked by your trials, tribulation or circumstances. Let your response to your circumstance move you forward. Don't dwell on the emotion of discouragement, anger, depression and doubt that come from your circumstances.

Identify the source of your circumstances.

When God is getting ready to blessed you all hell breaks out. It could be Satan trying to stop your blessing or it could be your own lack of knowledge of what God wants to do in your life. Or it could be your lack of knowledge on what to do or how to do what God is calling you to do. Whatever the problem is, you need to identify the source in order to move forward.

I can recall a time in my life when I experienced quite a bit of adversity over a short period of time. These obstacles came into my life when I was trying to act on what God was telling me to do. They came in the form of both large and small trials. I could have chosen to respond to these trials by quitting, turning around, taking a detour, getting angry, becoming frustrated and discouraged or simply slowing down. I chose to slow down and get frustrated; but, I did not quit. This meant I was still on the road to victory. As I began to work through my problems I needed to understand where they were coming from. Because of my relationship with God, the Holy Spirit gave me a check in my spirit that something more was going on. I started asking myself why I was experiencing so many problems and all at the same time. When I really thought about it and prayed about my problems, I realized that these problems were either from Satan or my lack of knowledge. However, this time it was not my lack of knowledge about God's plan for my life that was causing my problem, but it was Satan himself. It was Satan interfering with and trying to hinder God's plan for my life. When I realized that it was Satan hindering me, I rebuked him and his works and kept moving forward with God's plan. Jesus says that, *"The thief's purpose is to steal and kill and destroy. My purpose is to give life in all its fullness"* (*John 10:10, NLT*). Therefore, it is very important that you always know how the devil is working against you to get you out of God's plan for your life.

The scripture says that you should know Satan plans so that he will not outsmart you.

"So that Satan will not outsmart us. For we are very familiar with his evil schemes"(2 Corinthians 2:11, NLT).

The Holy Spirit will reveal Satan's schemes against you, if you ask Him. When you know Satan's plans, you can rebuke all his plans in the Name of Jesus. The scripture also says in the book of James that you can resist Satan and he will flee. The power of the Holy Spirit will help you resist Satan and God will give you an appropriate plan of action in the natural that will result in you getting the victory against the works of Satan.

Stand strong in the mist of your circumstances.

Ephesians says that, *"In every battle you will need faith as your shield to stop the fiery arrows aimed at you by Satan." Ephesians 6:16, NLT).* The devil throws these fiery darts which are attacks that comes one after another. Before we find a solution to one problem another problem comes. The Word says that we will have to have faith in order to withstand and stop the attack of Satan. We will have to stand our ground and never give up by continuing to slowly move forward or stand still knowing that God will see us through. If you don't know what the scripture says then you will get discouraged, angry, weary, depressed, worried, impatient, unbelieving and then you will quit. This is why it's so important to study the scripture, so you will know what to do in all circumstances.

When I was under a satanic attack, problem after problem was thrown at me yet, I kept moving forward toward a blessing that the Lord had for me. I never gave up! I never quit! I did not turn around! I did not get discouraged and I did not get angry. God explained to me what was happening and what I should do. I stood in faith, kept my eyes on Him and not on my problem.

Here's how my series of attacks unfolded:

1) The ice machine in my home broke down.
2) My husband's car required a new ignition.

3) We started having confusion among the staff in our business.
4) Robert, my husband, had a tooth ache and had to get a root canal.
5) My nephew got sick and had to be admitted to the hospital
6) Our son got sick in his body.
7) My husband's uncle died.
8) The Internal Revenue Service audited us.
9) My mother was worried and lonely.
10) One of the transmitters went out in our house.
11) Robert had to go to the hospital because his heart was racing.
12) Robert got nails in two tires on his new truck.

God gave me the victory in every situation. Now, these problems caused extra work and required me to spend money, but everything was solved, because God gave me the victory in every circumstance. God provided every single time. I passed the audit with the Internal Revenue Service without extra cost; Robert's heart was normal; my nephew got better and went home from the hospital; my mother was just feeling down for one day, but the next day she was fine; the ice machine was repaired, and Mr. Robert got the staff under control. Of course, these problems took a toll on me and caused me to move much slower. I became a bit frustrated, but I never quit and I never stopped or turned around. Instead of taking large steps of faith, I took smaller steps and pushed forward as hard as I could; because, I believed that God was with me. He never left me in my times of trouble. I also remembered the scripture that says, *"I can do all things through Christ which strengtheneth me" Philippians 4:13, KJV).* I knew in my heart that Jesus was carrying me and would deliver me from all of my distress, if I did not quit.

Even though these problems were a distraction and caused discomfort, I knew that my troubles would not last long so I figured that I could bear the discomfort for a little while. I stood on the previously mentioned scriptures, which helped me to push forward into God's blessings. I kept my eyes on Jesus; while, I moved forward into the blessings of the Lord and I received victory over the enemy.

Stay committed to God's plan.

God is committed to you and He takes care of you, because He is your Father and you are His child. **You must make God and his work a primary focus in your life.** If you would only trust Him and become fully committed to Him, He will deliver you from all of your troubles; not some, but ALL of your troubles. David says in *Psalm 37:5 "Commit everything you do to the Lord. Trust him, and he will help you."* When you are dedicated to God's plan, which involves having confidence in the way He chooses to resolve your situations, He gives you the desires of your heart. *"And he will give you all you need from day to day if you live for Him and make the Kingdom of God your primary concern"(Matthew 6:33 NLT).* Put God first in all you do and He will bless you and meet your every need. Stay focused on God.

Keep praising God in All Things.

We should believe and know that God can handle any and all of our problems and we should never let the bumps in the road of life stop us from praising the Lord. *"In everything gives thanks; for this is the will of God in Christ Jesus concerning you"(1Thessalonians 5:18 KJV).* We should give God thanks for every trial, large or small. We should believe and know in our hearts that God can handle any, and all of our problems. In the book of Matthew, Jesus teaches the multitude and the disciples about worry. He says *"And if God cares so wonderfully for flowers that are here today and gone tomorrow, won't he more surely care for you? You have so little faith"* (Matthew 6:30, NLT). Jesus cares for us and He says that we have little faith. Have faith in God; believe His word. He will surely take care of you.

You have to pray and believe that God will answer.

When we pray to God about our problems He hears us and He answers us. *Isaiah 65:24 says, "I will answer them before they even call to me. While they are still talking to me about their needs, I will go ahead and answer their prayers!"* God takes care of all our needs as we trust and let Him handle our problems. Remember, don't grow weary in well doing, because in due season you will be blessed if you don't quit.

Never give up, move forward.

You must stay focused and never give up. The blessings that God has planned for you are in the spiritual realm. They will manifest in your life if you keep believing God's words and never give up on the promises of God. All of your blessings that the Lord has for you are eternal and those blessings will last forever. So, when nothing seems to be working out for you, read your Bible, pray, and don't worry or concentrate on your problem; look to Jesus. Stay positive and refuse to doubt, believe that God will and can deliver you at any time, at any moment.

"God told me personally, 'that he can change my situation quicker than I could blink my eyes.' Hallelujah! What a word from the Lord. Remember that God is never late. As His children, we can always cry out to the Lord. *"I cried out to the Lord in my great trouble, and he answer me. I called to you from the world of the dead, and Lord, you heard me" (Jonah 2:2, NLT).* Jonah said that God heard him from the land of the dead. And guest what! You are not dead yet. Surely God hears you. God hears you when you cry out to Him and in His mercy and grace for you, he answers. David says *"the righteous cry and the Lord heareth and delivereth them out of all their troubles"(Psalm 34:17, KJV).* Guess what? God will deliver you too, and whatever your situation might be don't give up on God. Keep moving forward. Never give up on the vision or dream that God has given you. If you don't give up and remain faithfully moving ahead on what God told you, you will receive the victory. You don't need to look at your present situation or problems, look to Jesus. As you keep moving forward into the blessings of the Lord, then and only then will you get your victory. God is able to do it. God is the only one that is able to deliver you and change your situation. God will encourage you and give you the strength to continue on in your journey to keep you from giving up. In spite of our troubles, God is able to help us so that we will be victorious.

CHAPTER THREE

Moving Forward

Get Moving

We have established that God wants you blessed and now is the time to move forward. In chapter one, I talked about the promises of God and how to walk them out. Chapter two explains the different trials, tribulations and circumstances that come as you walk into your blessing and how to fight through them. Now, I will talk about the need to stand strong and move forward. In order to stand strong and move forward, you will need to clothe yourself in the full **Armor of God**. The full Armor of God is truth, righteousness, peace, faith, salvation, word of God, and prayer. When you operate with God's full armor you will be able to enter into God's rest and move forward into your blessing.

First, you must believe the **truth** of what God is communicating to you. The truth is that God loves you and wants you blessed. When you believe the truth, you have taken a step towards your blessing.

You must be **righteous.** You are made right with God by believing the works on the cross. You have been redeemed from sin. When you are righteous, good things come back to you. *"The godly are showered with blessings"(Proverbs 10:6, NLT).*

You must keep your **peace**. When the peace of God is upon you, you are capable of conquering the world. Your peace comes from knowing that God is with you and that He will fight your battle. This gives you strength to move forward because nothing can stand against you. *"I lay down and slept. I woke up in safety, for the Lord was watching over me"(Psalm 3:5, NLT)*.

You need strong **faith** in order to believe that God is with you. Psalms 16: 8 say that *"I know the Lord is always with me. I will not be shaken, for he is right beside me"*. Realizing that God is with you at every moment gives you the courage to move forward.

You need **salvation**. You need to know that God will deliver you out of all your troubles. *"The righteous face many troubles, but the Lord rescues them from each and every one"(Psalm 34:19, NLT)*. Yes, God will deliver you at the right time out of all circumstances, so that you can keep moving forward.

You need the **word** of God. You need to know his promises for you. You need to study and meditate on God's word. When you study the word of God it changes your thinking, it encourages you, and builds your faith. In the Word of God you will discover a plan that will keep you moving forward. God's instruction to Joshua was *"Study this Book of the law continually. Meditate on it day and night so you may be sure to obey all that is written in it. Only then will you succeed"(Joshua 1:8, NLT)*.

You need to **pray**. When you pray you are communicating with God. Luke 18:1 says, *"One day Jesus told his disciples a story to illustrate their need for constant prayer and to show them that they must never give up"*. It is safe to say without daily communication with God you will lose faith and quit. Continue to pray and believe so that you can enter into God's rest. The scripture says that God will surely give justice to his people who plead with him day and night. Don't give up and keep on moving forward.

Finally, **never get weary** in well doing. Stay focused on Jesus. If you don't grow weary you will reach your goal. You will receive the blessing that God has for you. That is why you keep moving forward to receive what God has for you. Galatians 6:9 says, *"So don't get tired of doing what is good. Don't get discouraged and give up, for we will reap a harvest of blessing at the appropriate time"*. Don't get tired; don't go backwards, but move forward into the blessing because you are clothed in the full **Amor of God.**

CHAPTER FOUR

Your Blessing Comes from Two Different Sources.

God Blessing in on You

Who blesses you? Did God give you your blessings or are you receiving your blessings from Satan? Do not be surprised. Satan blesses people. Look around at all the people that deny that Jesus is Lord, and you will see most of them do not live in poverty. They are actually blessed. But their blessing is not complete, and there will be an end to it. They live in constant fear of losing everything. Jesus blesses us out of love. Satan blesses his people out of deceit and hatred for mankind. Remember the scripture says that, *"The thief's purpose is to steal and kill and destroy. My purpose is to give life in all its fullness"(John 10:10, NLT)*. Satan blesses the people that serve him, so that they can use what they have to destroy God's people and God's kingdom. You do not want to be a part of what the devil is doing. So receive Christ as your Savior and serve God.

If God is the source of your blessing, then you are blessed whether you are obedient or disobedient because of God's mercy. Let me start off telling you that this was not the case in the Old Testament. God told the people that He would bless them if they would obey his law and regulations. God would bless them if they kept his commandments. The scriptures say, *"If you fully obey the Lord your God by keeping all the commands I am giving you today, the Lord your God will exalt you above all the nations of the world. You will experience all these blessings if you obey the Lord your God" (Deuteronomy 28: 1-2, NLT).* God also said, *"But if you refuse to listen to the Lord your God and do not obey all the commands and laws I am giving you today, all these curses will come and overwhelm you" (Deuteronomy 28: 15, NLT).* God promised to bless the people if they obey his commandments. So the people were blessed for a while; but, they were punished for their disobedience in the end. The people could not keep the commandments because of sin, and that is why God came up with a better plan and a new covenant. We live now under the new covenant.

The old covenant showed us that we were sinners, and the new covenant tells us that we are forgiven. Under the new covenant, we can be blessed by believing. What Christ did on the cross allows us to become children of God. The scripture says, *"When we were utterly helpless, Christ came at just the right time and died for us sinners. Now, no one is likely to die for a good person, though someone might be willing to die for a person who is especially good. But God showed his great love for us by sending Christ to die for us while we were still sinners. And since we have been made right in God's sight by the blood of Christ, he will certainly save us from God's judgment. For since we were restored to friendship with God by the death of his Son while we were still his enemies, we will certainly be delivered from eternal punishment by his life. So now we can rejoice in our wonderful new relationship with God all because of what our Lord Jesus Christ has done for us in making us friends with God all because of what our Lord Jesus Christ has done for us in making us friends of God" (Romans 5:6-11, NLT).* We are friends of God, and we are his dear children. The word goes on to say that since we are God's children we have received Christ's inheritance. We receive God's blessing, because we are His children. We can still be blessed by God while living in sin, because of his mercy for us. Just as we keep blessing our children when they do wrong; God does the same for us. We are forgiven for our sins because of what Christ did on the cross. We are delivered from eternal punishment. When we do sin, we repent and He forgives us keeping us in good **standing with**

him. God's forgiveness does not allow us to take advantage and keep living in sin, just the opposite. Christ died for our sin on the cross, and we died with him because we are one with Christ when we receive him as our Savior. *"Or have you forgotten that when we became Christians and were baptized to become one with Christ Jesus, we died with him? For we died and were buried with Christ by baptism. And just as Christ was raised from the dead by the glorious power of the Father, now we also may live new lives"*(Romans 6:3-4, NLT). Yes, we died to sin when we received Jesus Christ as our Savior. So, we cannot still live in sin. The scripture says, *"So, dear brothers and sisters, you have no obligation whatsoever to do what your sinful nature urges you to do. For if you keep on following it, you will perish. But if through the power of the Holy Spirit you turn from it and its evil deeds, you will live. For all who are led by the Spirit of God are children of God. So you should not be like cowering fearful slaves. You should behave instead like God's very own children, adopted into his family calling him "Father, dear Father". For his Holy Spirit speaks to us deep in our hearts and tells us that we are God's children. And since we are his children, we will share his treasures - for everything God gives to his Son, Christ, is ours, too. But if we are to share his glory, we must also share his suffering"*(Romans 8: 12-17, NLT). Since we died to sin when we received Jesus Christ as our Savior, then we should be living repented lives. We should turn from our sinful life and walk in righteousness; because, now we are children of God. Then we can share in everything that belongs to Christ which was given to him by his Father; the Father's blessing and suffering. We should turn from our sinful ways and follow Christ. But because of God's mercy and grace towards us, we can still be blessed and live in disobedience. Yes, we can still be blessed and still not walk in complete obedience to God, because of his mercy and his great love for us. Jeremiah says in the book of Lamentations 3:22-23 that, *"The unfailing love of the Lord never ends! By his mercies we have been kept from complete destruction. Great is his faithfulness; his mercies begin afresh each day"*. Because of God's mercy we are not totally destroyed. We get a chance to live and get it right. But when we do not get it right or walk in obedience, then we ask for forgiveness and change our behavior by repenting.

When we repent we turn around and go in a different direction. We do not keep that same sinful behavior, because we have received a righteous behavior. *"Instead, there must be a spiritual renewal of your thoughts and attitudes. You must display a new nature because you are a new person, created in God's likeness - righteous, holy and true"* *(Ephesians 4:23-24, NLT).* Our minds are being renewed day by day so that we can serve God. Paul tells the Colossians that, *"In its place you have clothed yourselves with a brand-new nature that is continually being renewed as you learn more and more about Christ, who created this new nature within you" (Colossians 3:10, NLT).* We received this new nature when we received Christ. So as we get to know Christ more by studying the Bible, we become righteous and stronger day by day because Christ lives in us and we live in him. You can choose to live a sinful life or choose to walk in obedience. If you choose to do the right thing, God will bless you. There is no condemnation for what we have done in the past. We have been forgiven, and we are made right with God by what Jesus Christ has done on the cross. We have become God's children, and we should behave like we are his children. And since we are God's very own children, we can come boldly to God's throne. The scripture says, *"So let us come boldly to the throne of our gracious God. There we will receive his mercy, and we will find grace to help us when we need it" (Hebrews 4:16, NLT).*

Because of God's mercy and his great love towards us, we can be blessed. We can receive God's blessing for our lives, and we can receive them right now. We receive God's blessing by believing God. We receive God's blessing by faith and faith in action. Our faith is made complete by what we do. **If you believe the word of God, show God that you believe his word by your actions.** Put into action what God has promised. Do not wait for the blessing to come to you. Move forward into what God has promised you. Let God be the source of where your blessing comes from. Then you can bless someone else.

CHAPTER FIVE

There is a Thin Line between Trust and Faith

Believe

There are three strong powers that influence us. One source is from God, one is from self, and one is from the devil. The three powers are trust, faith and unbelief. Remember what I said before, God comes to give life more abundantly and the devil comes to steal, kill and destroy. You have the choice to be on God's side or on the devil's side. I will explain the difference between trust, faith and unbelief and show you that faith is the power that God wants us to use. I will also talk about how faith in God will deliver you from all circumstances and move you into God's blessing.

First, let me define the three powers. The first of these is trust. **Trust** means to have a firm confidence, proof or evidence in the honesty, integrity, and reliability in a person or thing. **Faith** is confidence or unquestioning belief that does not require proof or evidence. And lastly, **unbelief** means to have a lack of belief because of insufficient evidence.

God wants to heal your body, break the yokes off your life, give you divine protection, build your relationships and bless you with abundance. All this requires a higher level of trust in God. **Moving from trust in God to faith in Him to deliver you is required**. Faith is the power that gets you your blessing. You can have all the trust you need, but without faith you will have nothing. Remember, trust requires evidence; faith does not. *"Faith is the confident that what we hope for will actually happen; it gives us assurance about things we cannot see"(Hebrews 11:1, NLT)*. Faith in God's ability to deliver is the power that makes you move into the impossible. *"For nothing is impossible with God"(Luke 1:37, NLT)*. It is not what you can do, but what God will do for you. You are not depending on self, but God for the deliverance. You know that all things are possible with God. That is why we don't look at the situation, but we stay focused on God's ability to deliver. We don't depend on our own ability, but we depend on God's ability. God is not a liar. He will deliver. *"And he who is the Glory of Israel will not lie, nor will he change his mind, for he is not human that he should change his mind" (1Samuel 15:29, NLT)*. God will deliver, and He will deliver you now. Not only trust God, but have faith in him to deliver.

Faith is the one power that moves mountains. The scripture says, *"Have faith in God, I assure you that you can say to this mountain, 'May God lift you up and throw you into the sea,' and your command will be obeyed. All that's required is that you really believe and do not doubt in your heart" (Mark 11: 22-23, NLT)*. Faith is the power that opens doors that no man can close. Faith in God's ability will flatten mountains and open doors for you and move you right into God's promises and blessings that He has ordained for you. Remember the definition of faith; it requires no physical proof or evidence to believe. You just have to believe God's word and that He is a delivering God that always wants the best for you. God is always on your side. *"I know that the Lord is always with me. I will not be shaken, for he is right beside me" (Psalms 16:8, NLT)*.

Unbelief was the problem for the Israelites. They did not enter the Promised Land because of unbelief. Even though Israel had evidence that God could save them, they did not trust the Father. They did not believe that God could deliver them from their troubles, so they perished in the wilderness. God did all sorts of miracles for them as they traveled to the Promised Land, and they were still in unbelief of his power to save and deliver them from all of their circumstances. God fed them manna from heaven, gave them water from a rock, and caused their clothes to never wear out. God fought their enemies, and kept them from sickness. God did all these things for them, but they would not believe that God would and could deliver them from the giants that were in the land that was theirs. In the past they had trusted God, but this was something different and harder. This was a new challenge. They thought that this new thing was too hard for God. Even though they had proof of God's past miracles, they had no trust. Although, they trusted God before and knew what he had done for them in the past, they did not trust Him with this new problem in their lives. They fell into unbelief. This is what we do. God delivers us out of all kinds of situations, and when a new trial comes into our lives we do not trust that He will do it again for us. Our mind or the devil tells us that God can't do this. It's too hard for God. Or we say that God won't do it for us, because he just got us out of trouble. Or we think that God is mad at us and won't save us because of our sin.

Our thoughts stop us from believing and trusting that God will help us, even though we have the proof and evidence that He will do it. Because of our unbelief, we miss out on the plan that God has for us. We do not enter into the promises or blessings that He has for us because of unbelief. We have the evidence of our past experiences, but we lack the evidence of God's word. We know now just as the Israelites knew about God's delivering power. **"I hear God saying, 'I can do it and I will do it for you now.'** God never changed his mind, He can and will deliver us. We should take those thoughts of unbelief and turn them around. We should cast those thoughts down and speak life into our situation. What would happen if we did that instead of not believing? What would happen, then? We would be filled with faith, believing that God can turn a situation around to work in our favor even though he hasn't dealt with that problem for us before. Mark 9:23 says, *"Jesus said unto him, if thou canst believe, all things are possible to him that believeth"*. We would believe God for his divine deliverance. We would have faith in God's abilities, not ours. Instead of going from trust to unbelief, go from trust to faith.

CHAPTER SIX

Your Lack of Faith Hurts Others

Obey!

God told me to clean my shower. Now, this is a job I hate; because, the shower is made of marble, and it is hard to clean when soap scum gets on it. So, I put some scrubbing bubbles on the shower (only the marble part), and then I went to do something else. I told myself that I would let it set for about fifteen minutes before coming back to clean. I needed to go outside to the garage to get a scrub brush; but then, I decided not to get a brush. I would just clean it with a towel. I figured it would have to do, because I did not feel like going outside in the cold weather. When I came back 20 minutes later the shower was clean. I was amazed; because, I did not have to scrub it. When I cleaned the shower before, I had to scrub it with a brush. But now I didn't need a brush to scrub the shower. I could just wash it down with a towel and then rinse. I was very happy about this and started to wipe the shower down. As I was wiping the shower, God started to speak to me. **"He said, 'See how clean your shower is. Maria has been keeping it clean, and she has done such a great job. All you have to do is wash it down without scrubbing it'. I said, 'Lord, she has been really cleaning my shower.'** Even though it did not look clean to me with the naked eye, she had really been cleaning it. It usually takes about forty-five minutes of scrubbing and wiping the shower to get is clean, but now it only took about ten minutes. **"God told me, 'Now call her to come back to clean your house.'**

You see I told her to stop coming; because, I did not have the funds to pay her at that time. God reminded me that it was not about me and He told me that she was saving her money to buy a car. She was depending on the money from me to purchase the car. God showed me this while I was doing a duty (cleaning the shower) that I did not like to do. He corrected my faith so I could help someone else. **"He said, 'You can't believe me for one hundred fifty dollars to pay her to clean your house?" I said, "Yes Lord.'** I have believed God for a lot more than one hundred fifty dollars. So I called Maria and told her to come back on her regular days to clean my house after God informed me that she was saving her money to purchase a car. She was using the monies from cleaning my house to do that. **"God also said, 'That when you make a decision based on a lack of faith, you don't only hurt yourself but others.'** God has a bigger plan. It is not all about you.

God is always working behind the scenes. When I looked at the shower, it did not look clean to me, but it was truly clean. I only noticed how clean it was when I had to clean it myself. God is working behind the scenes, and you don't even know or realize that He is working on your behalf. The scripture says God's ways and thoughts are higher than ours. *"My thoughts are completely different from yours," says the Lord. And my ways are far beyond anything you could imagine. For just as the heavens are higher than the earth, so are my ways higher than your ways and my thoughts higher than your thoughts"* (Isaiah 55:8-9, NLT). We don't know what God is doing, but God did not say that He wouldn't reveal it to us. He said that we have not, because we ask not. Ask, so that your joy can be full. *"Hitherto have ye asked nothing in my name, ask, and ye shall receive, that your joy may be full"* (John 16:24, KJV). We have to ask God to reveal his deep secrets to us. God revealed to me that He was helping Maria purchase a new car and that I interfered when I fired her from her job. God was helping Maria through me. She was saving her check every week from cleaning my house. I would look for her checks to clear my bank, but they never came through. She was saving my checks instead of cashing them, so that she would not spend the money. I ruined that too, because when I fired her, I told her not to hold my checks anymore, to cash them. God also told me that she was not cashing my checks so that she would not spend her money. Look what my lack of faith caused. She spent the money she had been saving for a car, because she cashed the checks. And you know how easy it is to spend cash. God had ordained the whole thing. My lack of faith ruined it. My correction from the Lord was to hire her back and pay her with cashier's checks. This would allow her to save her money to purchase her new car and my checkbook could stay balanced. God has a strange way of doing things.

While cleaning my shower, God showed me my lack of faith and the distress that my lack of faith caused someone else. God is in the blessing business. And when you don't have faith in God to take care of your needs, you hurt yourself and others, too. When God blesses, He blesses many people. **Your faith in God will help someone else, even when you don't see or realize it.** The money for cleaning my house that I did not have faith enough to believe God for was someone else's blessing. My blessing was a clean house; her blessing was a new car. Only the Holy Spirit can reveal such revelation to you. The scripture says that the Holy Spirit is the one that knows the mind of God and reveals things to your spirit. *"But we know these things because God has revealed them to us by his Spirit, and his Spirit searches out everything and shows us even God's deep secrets" (1 Corinthians 2: 10, NLT).* I never realized that I was blocking someone else's blessing. If I had asked God about getting rid of my housekeeper, he would have told me no. I could have prevented a lot of delays, extra work on my part and most of all stress, pain and inconvenience to Maria. *"Truly, O God of Israel, our Savior, you work in strange and mysterious ways"(Isaiah 45:15, NLT).* Our thoughts are not like his, and our ways are not like his.

Brenda Oglesby

God has a plan for us. We have to ask the Holy Spirit to reveal that plan to us so that we can walk in the path and the light that God has called us to walk in. We can't just go our own way, because what we do affects others without us knowing it. **Always ask God first before you make decisions on what to do.** He is just and faithful to guide you all the way. *"Trust in the Lord with all your heart; do not depend on your own understanding. Seek his will in all you do, and he will direct your path"* *(Provervs3:5-6, NLT).*

CHAPTER SEVEN

It's Mine

Claim It and Keep It!

My grandson, Jordan, had a habit of saying **'It's mine.'** I first heard Jordan proclaim "it's mine" when he was eighteen months old. The Webster Dictionary's definition of mine is that or those belonging to me. Now, if something belongs to you and only you, then it is yours. So when Jordan would say "it's mine", he was claiming what belonged to him.

One day while spending time with Jordan I started rubbing his feet. He immediately grabbed his feet and repeatedly declared **'It's mine'** and pulled his feet away from me declaring that they were his, and that I should not touch them. Jordon was making it clear that his feet belonged to him and no one else. Initially, I was slightly offended at his response; but, I remembered that his mother was teaching him to not let anyone touch him inappropriately or take what was his. So later on when I was getting Jordan ready for bed, I got his blanket for him and he shouted again, **'It's mine.'** When I touched his pillow, he once again let me know **'It's mine, keep your hands off, Grandma!'** When my husband, Robert, came home I shared Jordan's **'It's mine'** story with him describing how Jordan kept telling me **'It's mine Grandma'** and how he would remove my hand from everything I touched that belonged to him. We had a good laugh about Jordan clinging on to all that he knew belonged to him.

Jordan continued proclaiming *'It's mine'* for everything that belonged to him; but, then he started to claim things that did not belong to him. He started to claim things that he wanted to be his, even though, he knew they were not his possessions. He started claiming my things and his Grandpa things saying they were his. He even went so far as to put things in his closet that he knew did not belong to him. Just as I began to think that his behavior was a little strange, **"God spoke to me and said, 'Claim it and keep it.' And then He said, 'If something belongs to you and only you, then the devil do not have the right to try to take it from you.'**

God reminded me that we should all be like Jordan when it comes to our possessions and the devil. First, we should tell the devil, *'It's mine'* when he tries to take our blessing. Then like Jordan, we should declare that it is ours, rebuke the devil from touching our blessing and hold on to it. **"God also said, 'Don't let it go!'**

We should not let the devil convince us that our things belong to him. We should cast down every stronghold that he puts in our mind about our things belonging to him and about him destroying what we have. These strongholds come to us in our thoughts. The devil tries to convince us that we will be destroyed and that our enemies will overtake and kill us. He brings thoughts that we will live in poverty the rest of our lives and always be in debt. He brings thoughts that we will always be addicted to something or someone, and that we will never get free. He brings thoughts that our family will never receive salvation and that our relationships will fall apart. But I am here to tell you that he is a liar and a great liar. We have victory! We should take every evil thought and cast it down. Get rid of it. Replace every evil thought with good thoughts. Use your spiritual weapons to breakdown every evil thought that is not of God. The scripture says, *"We use God mighty weapons, not mere worldly weapons, to knock down the Devil's strongholds"* (2 Corinthians 10:4, NLT). We have to cast down all thoughts that are not of God. We do this by saying that we cast those thoughts down by faith and by speaking out scriptures that are contrary to what the devil is telling us. We read and confess scriptures on prosperity, healing and deliverance. We read and confess scriptures on the blessing of the Lord. We read and confess scriptures on having faith in God to deliver us at all times. We know and believe that all things are possible with God. We not only read and claim these scriptures, but we *believe* that God can and will do them in our lives.

So when I touched Jordan's feet, he immediately told me that his feet were off limits by what he said and by what he did. This is what we should do to the devil when he attacks our bodies...our finances...our families...our relationships and our lives. We should tell him to get his hands off and we should push him away. We push the devil away by putting on the whole Armor of God, by living righteously, praying, calling out scriptures that contradict what the devil is saying to us and by casting down evil thoughts. We must believe in God's ability to deliver us. We demonstrate and strengthen our belief by receiving God's word that says healing and blessings belongs to us in every area of our lives and that the devil does not have the right to take it away. We can find healing and blessing scriptures in the Bible that deal with any situation that we might have. Claim them over yourself daily. We must seek out people of faith to stand in agreement with us for our healing and blessing and believe that God will heal our lives.

Jordan never backed away from telling me, **'It's mine.'** Likewise we should never back away from claiming that perfect healing and blessings in every area of our lives. Jordan never gave me the opportunity to rub his feet. I had to remove my hands from his feet before he got angry and started to cry. We should never give the devil the opportunity to touch our bodies, our finances, our families, our relationships or anything that belongs to us. We should get angry and get ready for battle. Never let the devil get the upper hand in your life. When you first recognize that he is trying to take something from you, start your battle then, not later. As a matter of fact you should be ready at all times before something happens. You will surely win.

Since the devil has the nerve to attack you, then you attack him. Not only do you stop him from taking what belongs to you, but take what he has. That's right! Take what the devil has just like when Jordan took what belonged to him and what belonged to me also.

"God told me, 'Look at your grandson; he not only wanted what was his, but he wanted yours too.'"

When the devil comes in to claim what is yours, stop him in his tracks. Take what he has; don't let him take what you have. Keep your stuff and get his too. The word says that the devil has to pay back seven fold when he steals from us. *"But if he is found out, he must restore seven times what he stole; he must give the whole substance of his house if necessary to meet his fine". (Proverbs 6:31, Amp).* Therefore, claim and call out more than he took or is trying to take from you. If he took one hundred dollars, then you tell the devil he needs to pay you back seven hundred dollars. If the devil makes you sick in your body, then you claim complete healing for yourself and for seven other people. If the devil breaks up your marriage, then you claim your marriage be mended and seven other marriages be mended, also. If the devil gets you addicted, then you claim that seven people with addiction be set free. Do you understand what I am saying? Pray for seven fold blessings. This will shut the devil up and start him running the other way. He will stay away for a season.

You have to be smarter than the devil. Never give him the upper hand. Always stay prayed up and full of the word. Clothe yourself with the full Armor of God to stop the works of the devil. *"Use every piece of God's armor to resist the enemy in the time of evil, so that after the battle you will still be standing firm"(Ephesians 6:13, NLT).* When you are still standing after the battle you know that you have won. When we put on Gods' full armor, we can fight against the devil and win. When we trust God and believe that He is working on our behalf, we win. We get victory every time. So, never give in or give up! You will win. *"So don't get tired of doing what is good. Don't get discouraged and give up, for we will reap a harvest of blessing at the appropriate time" (Galatians 6:9, NLT).* Fight for your stuff and take what the devil has, too!

CHAPTER EIGHT

Are you in Hell Yet?

Let's Get Out!

Are you in hell yet? If not you will go there one day. It is your worst day when nothing goes right; everything you do turns out wrong; whatever you say is wrong; it's the wrong time, wrong seasons, wrong day, and the wrong hour, even the minute and all odds are against you. Nothing goes right and whatever you touch turns into disaster. It is the day your loved one dies; you lost your job; your business; your finances were all lost. It is the day you lost all your possessions (home, automobile, boat, jewelry) your retirement money. It is the day you became sick with (cancer, diabetes, loss of limbs, blindness, or lost your hearing). It is the day you went to prison; it is your worst day. It is the day when you are between a rock and a hard place. No one can help and no one can save you, but God can save you. *"When you're in over your head, I'll be there with you. When you're in rough waters, you will not go down. When you're between a rock and a hard place it won't be a dead end. Because I am God, your personal God, the Holy of Israel, your Savior"* (Isaiah 43:2-3, Message). When you are in that hard place, you will say, Lord just kill me and let me come home with you so I won't have to face this problem or situation any longer. You tell God, I'd rather die and be with you than have this problem and this trouble. But God does not speak. You look up to heaven for him to take you right now, but nothing happens. The day gets worse. You start having one problem after another. It's just like the scripture says, that Satan is at work against you throwing those fiery darts one after another. And he is hitting his target "you" every time. Before you receive one problem, another one comes just as quickly. I did not say before you fix one problem, another one comes. I said before you receive one problem another one appears. You do not have time to adjust to the first problem before the second, third, fourth and more come your way. You are stressed and full of despair. You don't know which way to turn or go. You turn to the left and it is bad. You turn to the right and it is worse than the left. I will turn around and dig a hole in the floor to disappear into, you say to yourself. What will you do? What will you say? Where will you go? There is no way out. There is nowhere to go. You are trapped. There is no one to help you; no one you can turn to. You don't want to ask family or friends. You don't want them to know that you're in trouble; you don't want to bother them; they just will not understand. And if they did understand or wanted to help they can't help you anyway. You can't go to the bank. They won't help you, unless you are perfect. They don't want to take a risk on you. But God! You are at your limit on your credit card. You can't borrow anymore and your credit has gotten so bad that neither the bank nor any lending institution can help you. You can't get help at the church they want to know your life history in order to help you. And most of the time they will not help, because they can't pay bills, buy food and clothing for everyone that asks, because then they will go broke. Most churches won't help because that is their policy; they have a limit on what they'll do in their care ministry for needy families. Then, if you ask or even if they do help you, you will be the gossip of the church.

So where do you turn? Who do you turn to? You turn to God the Deliverer and the salvation of our soul. God can save us. He is the great "I AM". He can save us from all destruction. "The *unfailing love of the Lord never ends! By his mercies we have been kept from complete destruction*" (Lamentations 3:22, NLT). Yes, because of God's mercy toward us we have been kept from complete destruction. When you are between a rock and hard place God will keep you stable and secure. Isaiah 33:6 says, *"God keeps your days stable and secure - salvation, wisdom, and knowledge in surplus, and best of all, Zion's treasure, Fear- of-God"(Isaiah 33:6, Message)*. God will keep us secure, stable and safe and He will deliver us from our troubles. *"The righteous face many troubles, but the Lord rescues them from each and everyone" (Psalm34:19, NLT)*. In the time of trouble God will and can deliver us. God loves us and He wants to help us. God is not like people. He is different. No matter what mess you are in, no matter how bad the situation is, no matter how sick you are, God wants to help you. Even when you can't see a way out, God has a plan for you. He is working it out even when we can't fathom it or even see it. In reality it looks like you are going down. You are going down to hell. But I tell you, you are not going to **fail,** you will not be **overtaken,** but you will have **victory;** if you put your trust in the one that saves you. And that one is the Lord himself. No enemy will overtake you, no situation will conquer you, no sickness will kill you, and neither man nor nation is stronger than the Lord.

If you trust in the Lord, God says in Psalms that he would steady us and make us strong. That our enemies will not get the best of us, nor will the wicked overpower us. Don't depend on anything else but the Lord. In the right time and season, He will deliver you from all destruction. Before you even ask the Lord, He will deliver you. He already knows that you need help and He is able and willing to help you. James *says, "Whenever trouble comes your way, let it be an opportunity for joy (James1:2, NLT)*. Yes, count it all joy, because the Lord will help you in a time of need. *"For nothing is impossible with God"(Luke 1:37 NLT)"*. All things are possible with him. Depend on him and He will deliver you at the right time. And it will not be late; it will be when you're at the end of your ropes; when you can't see or know how you are going to make it. The moment you surrender all and put your hope and faith in the Lord, He will come. When you acknowledge and say God, if you don't deliver me, then I will be completely destroyed. Then I know God will hear your cry, because you put your trust totally in him. And suddenly God will be there before you can blink your eyes. And the Lord will say to you I did not forget you, you will not fail; you will not go to hell. I am going to make all things new. So, don't let Satan tell you that God is not coming, that he will not save you. Trust God and wait upon him, He will never fail you. *"But the Lord still waits for you to come to him so he can show you his love and compassion. For the Lord is a faithful God. Blessed are those who wait for him to help them (Isiah30:18, NLT)*. Keep the same attitude and declaration that the Shunammite woman had (2 Kings 4: 8-36). "Keep saying 'all is well,' Keep on saying 'everything is fine.'

"God says that, 'Even though everything was dying around her she kept saying, "all is well, everything is just fine.' And I can take what was dead and turn it back into life.'"

When all things look like it is at the end for you, say to yourself "all is well" and keep moving on. **Because God can change your situation before you can blink your eyes.** He can take what the devil meant for evil and turn it into good. The Lord can and will change your situation. Those who wait upon the Lord He will renew their strength and God can renew your strength right now. In due season, you will have what you have been waiting for and the good part of all this is; God will not be late. He is always right on time. Solomon says, *"God has made everything beautiful for its own time" (Ecclesiastes 3:11, NLT)*.

CHAPTER NINE

Afflicted But Not Defeated

Who Cares What the Circumstance Is?

My grandbaby, Jordan, got bitten by a mosquito on the right side of his face above his eye. Jordan is allergic to mosquito's bites. So, when he got bitten the entire right side of his face was swollen to the point that his right eye closed shut. Because he could not attend daycare I had the opportunity to keep him that week. You know how grandmothers are - my plan was to nurse him back to health. This happened to him on a Sunday night, and I went to his home early Monday morning to pick him up. As we were driving home, I cried because it hurt me to my heart to see him in such bad condition. He kept looking at me with that one eye and it was just unbearable for me. All the way home I kept telling him it's going to be fine and that he was going to be alright. I had already decided that Jordan would lie down when we arrived at my house and I would give him his medication and everything would be fine. Well, little did I know Jordan wanted to play. Jordan started to run, climb, and jump. Jordan was doing what a healthy two year old does. I said to myself that Jordan is more active sick, than when he is not sick. As I watched Jordan in full action, **"The Holy Spirit said to me, 'Afflicted, But Not Defeated.' "My reply was, 'what did you say,' "the Holy Spirit repeated himself and said, 'Afflicted, But Not Defeated.' "The Holy Spirit went on to say, 'Look at your**

grandbaby. He is in full form. He has never stopped. Even though he can only see out of one eye he has not let that stop him. He is doing more now than he did when he had two eyes. And he does not even know that he is in distress.'

Jordon did not even know that he was afflicted but I knew, and I felt the pain that he was not having. There is a lesson to learn from this. Jordan was afflicted but not defeated. Affliction hit his life, but that did not stop him from moving forward. With the affliction he was doing more than he did without the affliction. Now here is the word! **"The Holy Spirit said, 'This is how we need to act. We need to duplicate what Jordan did. When we are afflicted we need to keep going and never give up. We need to do more or push harder when we have times of difficulty and distress.'**

Jordan was my example. Jordan not only acted like himself, but he also acted like he was not hurting, he kept playing, laughing and having fun. He was not mad because he could not see. Jordan did not even notice that he was afflicted. In Jordon's eyes everything was normal. To him, nothing was wrong. I was the one worrying about him. I was the one that noticed he had only one good eye and I was feeling sorry for him. I was the one who thought he was helpless. Jordon showed no sign of distress, worry, or hurt. He did not even want to sit down and relax with only one good eye. And most of all, he did not notice that he had been afflicted. Jordan kept on being Jordan. His only plan was to do what he always does and more of it. This was just a normal day to him, a day to play. It was amazing to watch Jordan play. It was as though he had the use of both of his eyes. **"And the Holy Spirit said to me, 'Watch him!' This is what I expect you to do when trouble and tribulations come your way. Jordan is happy and having fun. He is not worried about anything and he is not worried about his eye. This is how I want you and others to act when affliction comes your way. Count it all joy.'** *"Whenever troubles come your way, let it be an opportunity for joy. For when your faith is tested, your endurance has* *a chance to grow. So let it grow, for when your endurance is fully developed, you will be strong in character and ready for anything"(James1:2-4NLT).* Be happy when you have troubles, don't complain, don't get angry, don't worry, and please don't quit. Just keep on moving forward and do as Paul advised in the book of First Corinthians ninth chapter. Practice self – control and run straight toward your goal even if you have afflictions, trials, troubles, or tribulations. Cast down all things that that can hold you back from victory. Cast down all things that are not from our Heavenly Father. Run this race with joy expecting God to do a miracle in your life. Don't worry about anything, but pray about all things. Keep a good attitude and keep moving forward. Duplicate what Jordan did. He kept playing, running, jumping and having fun. He did not quit what he was doing just because he was afflicted. And we too must never quit because tribulations come our way. We must do like Jordan did and keep going. We must move forward, never quitting. This is how God the Father wants us to act. When affliction comes upon us we should not let it stop us in our tracks; we should be like Jordan never noticing that we have an affliction and keep moving. When we do this we will and can identify with Christ. The scripture says, *"He was oppressed and treated harshly, yet he never said a word. He was led as a lamb to the slaughter. And as a sheep is silent before the shearers, he did not open his mouth"(Isaiah 53:7, NLT).* We should be like Christ. He suffered for us and did not say a word so that we could be accepted by God as his children. Since we are God's children the word says, *"And since we are his children, we will share his treasures for everything God gives to his Son, Christ, is ours too. But if we are to share his glory, we must also share his suffering"(Romans 8:17, NLT).* Yes, we are God's children and we have to suffer sometimes too. But remember if we never quit and hold on to God's promise we will get the reward that the Father has promised us and we will get the victory in all things.

When we are afflicted, we should not complain. The affliction that we go through will not last long. During the times of our suffering, we should learn and understand what God is doing and saying to us. God could be building our character, strengthening us, trying to move us in a different direction, or correcting us. But whatever it is, just know that He is getting us ready. Our suffering is for a set time. *"For our present troubles are quite small and won't last very long. Yet they produce for us an immeasurably great glory that will last forever! So we don't look at the troubles we can see right now; rather, we look forward to what we have not yet seen. For the troubles we see will soon be over, but the joys to come will last forever"(2 Corinthians 4:17-18, NLT).* Our time of affliction is for a set time and will end soon. When the trouble is over, the blessing comes. This is what brings you joy. Can you hold out and wait for the Lord to bring you through? God is with you in your suffering. He is right beside us. He never leaves us. He helps us in our time of affliction. So, you do not go through your troubles alone. God is with you. The Holy Spirit is there comforting you, guiding you, directing the activities of your life, advising you and keeping you safe. And the scripture says. *"We are pressed on every side by troubles, but we are not crushed and broken. We are perplexed, but we don't give up and quit. We are hunted down, but God never abandons us. We get knocked down, but we get up again and keep going"* Corinthians4:8-9, NLT). That's right we keep on going just like the scripture says never giving up. We should follow the example of my grandbaby. We keep going on with full force, never quitting and counting it all joy until we get the victory.

Chapter Ten

You have Fallen

But You Have the Victory!

I am reminded of the story about the eagle and his children. How the father eagle teaches his children to fly. You see, at a certain time the father eagle stirs the nest and throws his children out of the nest. The young birds are frightened and flapping their wings desperately trying to survive while falling to the ground. But the father eagle watches and just before they hit the ground he comes down with his large wings and scoop the eaglets upon his large wings and brings them to safety. This is what our Father does to us sometimes. He waits until the last minutes to save us from disaster. He always waits until the last minute to help us. We know in our hearts that if only God will intervene on our behalf we would be fine. But day after day, week after week, month after month and year after year there is no help from our Father. You say, "Where are you? When will you come? When will you help? Father if you don't help I will be destroyed." But He still does not come to your rescue. You just keep holding on and waiting for him to deliver you. Have you ever felt this way? I have felt like this plenty of times and I feel like this now. I know deep down in my heart that God will save me from destruction, but when will he do it? And God says to my heart, *"We are pressed on every side by troubles, but we are not crushed and broken. We are perplexed, but we don't give up and quit. We are hunted down, but God never abandons us. We get knocked down, but we get up again and keep going" (2Corinthians4:8-9, NLT).* Even though we go through these hard times God never leaves us. God goes through these hard times with us. He is with us so we won't fail. And He is there to deliver us at the right time.

You might say, why do we have to go through hard times? There are many reasons we go through hard times. But whatever the reason is, remember that God loves you and there is always a lesson to learn and you should ask God what is He saying to you or trying to teach you. Don't question God with why, but ask God to teach you so that you might learn and not have to go through this again. Then let God know that, "I want to please you and I have faith in your ability to save me. Please help me through this trial." With this kind of attitude you cannot and will not lose. You will not be a victim, but a winner. No bitterness, no anger, no depression, nor pity will come in your heart and cause you to experience pain and defeat. *"Whenever trouble comes your way, let it be an opportunity for joy. For when your faith is tested, your endurance has a chance to grow. So let it grow for when your endurance is fully developed you will be strong in character and ready for anything"(James1:2-4, NLT).* Then you will be able to go through trials with joy and this shows God that you have faith in him to deliver. You are showing God that you are not depending on self, but on his mighty power to deliver and save you from destruction. Your season will come because there is a time for everything. And your time will come soon. *"You sent troops to ride across our broken bodies, we went through fire and flood, but you brought us to a place of great abundance" (Psalm 66:12, NLT).* You might believe that it is your time now. But what is God saying? What is God trying to teach you? What is missing? Are you doing something wrong? No, you just might be waiting on God's perfect timing. God knows the right time to bless you. And when He does you will forget all the times that you wished for Him to come. You will forget the hard times and tribulations that you went through; because, God will make all things new right before your eyes. You will remember how you almost fell, but before you hit bottom God picks you up at the right time and save you. Just like the father eagle scoops up his children before they hit the ground and bring them back into the nest.

At the right time God will scoop us up and bring us back to safety. The eagle was only teaching his children how to fly. He loves his children and he meant them no harm. Just as the eagle loves his children, God loves us. When we go through tribulations, God is teaching us. During those times we need to ask the Father 'What is my lesson? Reveal it to me so I can learn what you are teaching me.' If God is not teaching you something, then He wants you to wait upon him to work out the details of what He is doing. God is not only trying to bless you, but a group of people. So there might be a lot of details that God has to work out. But remember God has not forgotten you; he is working on your behalf. God sets things straight and moves things around for our benefit so that we can have the best blessing in every area of our lives.

The blessing I am talking about is something supernaturally happening in your life. Not something that's mediocre, but something so great that we know only God could ever make it happen. So just hold on and remember that great tribulations can come right before a great blessing. Be like David when he said 'God, my future is in your hands please rescue me from my enemies.' We should believe like David that whatever our circumstances may be, God is still sitting on the throne and He has a set time for our deliverance. And when that time comes all hell better watch out for our all powerful God. The scripture says if you partake in my blessing you have to partake in my suffering. As long as we live on the earth there will be times of suffering and times of victory; but, we have to keep our faith in God because He is with us. And if we keep faith in God's perfect timing we will get the victory every time. "Job said, *"Why seeing times are not hidden from the Almighty does He not set seasons for judgment? Why do those who know Him not see His days for punishment of the wicked? (Job 24:1, Amp).*"**God is saying now, 'don't you understand, don't you see? Oh, how my people perish for lack of knowledge.**

49

Don't you know that I have a set time for everything? There is a time for judgment and a time for blessing. And when the time comes I will fulfill it all. So why do you weep? Why do you get frustrated? Don't weep, don't get frustrated or angry but believe me. I am a delivering God and I will come to visit you at the right time. The time of your visitation is not yet; but, soon it will come and not tarry. And you will forget the days and times that you looked for me and could not find me. I will not be late I will be right on time for your complete deliverance. So get up and count all of you tribulations as joy; because, you now know that your time will come soon and it will not be late.' God spoke this to me as I was writing. This is a prophecy to you; believe and receive the word of the Lord. Hallelujah to the Father Most High! for your words of deliverance. God's times are not hidden. God sets the right time. We have to wait on God's perfect timing. So, deal with the trials in your life, because they will not last long. The scriptures say, *"So we don't look at the troubles we can see right now rather we look forward to what we have not yet seen. For the troubles we see will soon be over, but the joys to come will last forever"(2Corinthians4:18, NLT).* In just a little while the trails or troubles will be over. Our tribulation will not last very long. We will soon have victory, because we walk by faith, not by sight. *"We will live by believing and not by seeing" (2 Corinthians 5:7, NLT).* So learn to be patient and wait on God's perfect timing for your victory.

CHAPTER ELEVEN

God Loves You

But He Wants You to Change

No matter what your circumstance is or what you have done in the past, God still loves you. If you are living in sin, God still loves you. It doesn't matter what you have done in the past or what you are planning to do in the future, God still loves you. If you are a homosexual, prostitute, murderer, adulterer, liar, alcoholic, drug addict, a racist, or you're just living in sin; Guess what! God still loves you. God loves you; He wants to bless you and He wants to help you. God loves us unconditionally with no strings attached. God is not like us. Sometimes, our love for others is conditional. I love you, but! **The Holy Spirit empowers us to love the way God loves**. We must ask the Holy Spirit to help us love unconditionally so that we can demonstrate God's love to the world.

Because of God's mercy, grace and unfailing love for us, we are kept from complete destruction even when we sin. God still loves us. The wages of sin are death and without repentance you will be punished. God wants us happy and as a loving Father He wants us blessed. In the Old Testament, God's blessing was based on being obedient to his commandments, his laws, and his precepts. To receive God's blessing he required that you walk in obedience to his word. God made a covenant with Israel and in that covenant they were blessed for being obedient; but if they were disobedient they were cursed. *"Today I am giving you the choice between a blessing and a curse! You will be blessed if you obey the commands of the Lord your God that I am giving you today. You will received a curse if you reject the commands of the Lord your God" (Deuteronomy 11:26, NLT).* God blessed Israel for a while, but after they continued to sin, He punished them. Even though Moses encouraged the children of Israel to choose righteousness so that they might live a long life full of God's blessings; they were obedient at times and at other times they were disobedient. During the times of obedience they were blessed and during the times of disobedience they were cursed. In the end, they were punished completely for their sins and sent away into captivity.

Now today, we live under a new covenant with the Lord. God has given us a new heart that we might obey him. It was hard for Israel to keep God's covenant, and today it is hard for us to keep God's covenant on our own. God gave us a new covenant in Christ so that we might be saved. This new covenant gives us a chance to have a personal relationship with God. God's commandants, laws, and precepts are to be in our hearts. God told Jeremiah, *"But this is the new covenant I will make with the people of Israel on that day, says the Lord, I will put my laws in their minds, and I will write them on their hearts. I will be their God, and they will be my people"(Jeremiah 31:33NLT).* With this new covenant, we can be blessed by God. God will forgive our sins and never again remember them. *"I yes I alone am the one who blots out your sins for my own sake and will never think of them again" (Isaiah 43:25, NLT).* With this new covenant God will not remember our sins and we have a chance to be blessed by God. We now live under God's grace and we get another chance if we mess up. **If we break God's commandants, laws, and precepts then we can still be blessed because of God's grace towards us. Since God will still bless us this does not give us permission to continue to sin.** You will still be accountable for the sins you commit in the midst of God blessing you. Not only did God make a way to forgive our sins with his new covenant; but He also made a way for us to receive salvation.

We have a chance to have eternal life if we believe in Christ and the works that he did on the cross. Because of what Christ did on the cross, we are set free from sin and we get a second chance with God. So now when God looks at us and what we have done, He sees his perfect sacrifice in his Son's blood. Christ's blood has paid the price for our sins. This is why we as sinners can have a perfect life and be blessed by God. Paul says it like this; *"Since God did not spare even his own Son but gave him up for us all, won't God, who gave us Christ, also give us everything else" (Romans 8:32, NLT).* This is God's redeeming grace towards us. God will not withhold anything we need to live for him and to be blessed by him. That is why you see so many people living in sin and they are still blessed. **God does not approve of what they are doing but, He loves us and out of mercy and grace for his people He blesses us anyway.**

God has done such wonderful things for us and we as his children should love him and try our best to walk in obedience. Remember the scripture says the wages of sin is death. You might have salvation and go to heaven, **but you will be held accountable for what you have done in this lifetime even though God has forgiven you.** God explains this in the Book of Revelation, *"And the book was opened, including the Book of Life. And the dead were judged according to the things written in the books, according to what they had done" (Revelation 20:12, NLT). We will be punished for what we have done during our lifetime.*

In the Old and New Testament is shows clearly that God patiently waits for us to change and when we do not change from our sinful behavior, He punishes us. This is what happened to the Amorites in the book of Genesis chapter fifteen. God had promised Abraham the land in Canaan which belonged to the Amorites. God told Abraham, *"After four generations your descendants will return her to this land, when the sin of the Amorites has run its course" (Genesis 15:16, NLT).* In other words, God was giving the Amorites time to get right with him. After four hundred years, the Amorites did not change from their sinful behavior and they lost their land to Abraham's descendants.

Another example is Paul's violent persecution of Christians. God in his mercy changed Paul and used him to proclaim the Good News to the Gentiles. *"But then something happened! For it pleased God in his kindness to choose me and call me, even before I was born! What underserved mercy!"(Galatians 1:15, NLT).* Paul did change and he had the opportunity to write fourteen books of the New Testament. He established many churches and was a great Apostle. God gave Paul another chance to serve him and He blessed him mightily. This scripture also shows that God has a plan for us and He knows before-hand what we will and will not do. It also shows that God is loving, kind and merciful in his dealings with his children. David is yet another example of God's grace and mercy. He was a great man and made many mistakes. But when he repented, God forgave him and blessed him greatly. There are so many other examples in the Bible of people that God showed mercy and grace to by restoring and blessing them even when they sinned. This is how God works. God gives us plenty of chances to repent.

Let me give you an additional example of what I mean by God's saving grace thru Christ Jesus. God is like our loving parents that continuously love us and give us chance after chance when we mess up. Our parents love us regardless of what we do, what we say, or what trouble we get ourselves into. Even when they do not approve of our bad behavior; but, it does not make our parents love us less nor bless us less. Our parents will still help us with our needs and love us. It is the same with God. He still loves us even when we sin and He will bless us just as a loving parents would, because he is merciful. **Even though we are under a new covenant we will still be punished for our sins.** God's word in the Bible is true and He will not go back on his word. He will fulfill everything he has said. *"Cursed is anyone who does not affirm the terms of this law by obeying them"* (Deuteronomy 27:26, NLT). And Deuteronomy 28:2 says, *"You will experience all these blessings if you obey the Lord your God"*. God is not a God that he shall lie. In his holiness, He cannot and will not lie. *"No, I will not break my covenant; I will not take back a single word I* *said. I have sworn an oath to David, and in my holiness I cannot lie"* (Psalm *89:34-35, NLT).* God loves us and whatever behavior you portray is what you will receive in return from the Lord.

God gave me a revelation about people confusing God's unfailing love for them and them representing him to the people. This is where many people misunderstand God's revelation about his love. God loves us in our sin, but we can't identify or have a close relationship with Him if we are not holy but, God still loves us. In order to **identify** with God and to **represent** Him, you have to walk in **holiness.** In order to have an **intimate** relationship with the Father, and **imitate** the Father you have to walk in **holiness**. God loves us unconditionally and that will never change. Apostle Paul says, *"And I am convinced that nothing can ever separate us from his love. Death can't and life can't. The angels can't, and the demons can't. Our fears for today, our worries about tomorrow, and even the powers of hell can't keep God's love away. Whether we are high above the sky or in the deepest ocean, nothing in all creation will ever be able to separate us from the love of God that is revealed in Christ Jesus our Lord"* (Romans 8:38-39, NLT). Therefore, if we walk in obedience or disobedience, God still loves us and He still blesses us. Walking in obedience leads to a purified life. Now, when you walk in holiness you can be intimate with God and you can identify with Him. God loves you, even if you are living in sin.

God commands that you be holy because he is holy. *"You must be holy because I, the Lord your God, am holy"* (Leviticus 19:2, NLT). **If you do not live a holy life, then you will become separated from God.** The book of Hebrews says, *"Try to live in peace with everyone, and seek to live a clean and holy life, for those who are not holy will not see the Lord"* (Hebrews 12:14, NLT). **You will become separated from God because of your ungodliness. While living an ungodly life, you cannot be a representative of who God truly is. God's holiness provides us with a pattern in which we can imitate what He does. So if you are a homosexual; God still loves you. Your sin is not greater than any other sin; because, God loves sinners. But, you are not holy and you cannot**

represent God to others, because of your ungodliness. Again, the scripture says, *"Ye shall be holy: for I the Lord your God am holy" (Leviticus 19:2, KJV).* **"And God said 'this has nothing to do with grace. This is a command.'** Living a holy life means to be separated from ungodliness and devoted to serving God. You should be separated from the evil activities of the world. Apostle James says, "You *adulterers! Don't you realize that friendship with this world makes you an enemy of God?" (James 4:4, NLT).* Follow the ways of God and don't be lured by what the world says is right. The world will have you doing things that are not right and unholy in God's eyes. Sin always blocks our view of God. If we want to see God for who He really is we have to keep ourselves separated from a sinful life style. **Holiness requires us to keep our mind, our soul and our heart free from corruption. Obedience requires us to keep the commandants, laws, and precepts written in the bible.**

We have established that God loves us no matter what. In order to walk in obedience and to be holy before God, we must keep God's commandments. When you defile your body with lust, sex outside of marriage, alcohol abuse, drugs and any other abuse that defiles the temple of God, you are not holy. *"Or don't you know that our body is the temple of the Holy Spirit, who lives in you and was given to you by God? You do not belong to yourself, for God bought you with a high price. So you must honor God with your body" (1 Corinthians 6:19, NLT).* Yes, your body is God's temple and you must keep it holy because God can not dwell in an unclean temple. We keep our body holy by renewing our minds. When our minds are renewed we represent God by the way we live. *"Don't copy the behavior and customs of this world, but let God transform you into a new person by changing the way you think. Then you will know what God wants you to do, and you will know how good and pleasing and perfect his will really is"(Romans 12:1, NLT).* Therefore, your mind has to be renewed so that you can walk in God's perfect will for your life. When you are in God's perfect will He can bless you. We can receive a blessing from the Lord when we walk in obedience to his word and live holy lives.

In Psalms 32:8 (NLT), *the Lord says," I will guide you along the best pathway for your life. I will advise you and watch over you."* God will guide us in our entire decision making. We will never have to wonder what God wants us to do or where He wants us to go. When we serve Him with our whole heart totally devoted to Him, He will help us completely. Jehovah will be a sure foundation for us, giving us complete salvation. At the right time, Jehovah will hear us and succor us. God requires you to renew your mind. You can renew your mind by studying, meditating, and doing what the Bible says. The Bible teaches you how to live a pure life. The Holy Spirit is your guide to help you become like God. When you are like Christ you can identify with him and represent him as a child of God. Don't be confused about what God wants from you. God loves you, but He wants you to walk in obedience and holiness. God wants us to represent him and that means walking holy before him. The word says, *"If you love me, obey my commandments" (John 14:15, NLT).* You hear that! What a powerful word. God says you show him that you love him by obeying his commandments. Learn your Bible and you will know at all times what God expects of you and then you can imitate him. The Bible is our teacher and the Holy Spirit will guide, lead, and help you keep God's commandants. You cannot keep God commandants on your own. You need help and that help comes from the Holy Spirit. *"But when the Father sends the Counselor as my representative - and by the counselor I mean the Holy Spirit, he will teach you everything and will remind you of everything I myself have told you" (John14:26, NLT).*

Renew your mind today. Make a choice to study and meditate on the Bible daily. What you read and meditate on will get deep down into your spirit and change you. One day, you will not want to do the things you use to do anymore. *"Don't copy the behavior and customs of this world, but let God transform you into a new person by changing the way you think. Then you will know what God wants you to do, and you will know how good and pleasing and perfect his will really is"(Romans 12:2, NLT).* Yes, with a renewed mind you can walk in holiness.

For God himself said, you must walk in holiness. And when you walk in holiness you will be blessed by God. God is a rewarder and He will reward you for your obedience. Whether it is good behavior or bad behavior you will be rewarded or punished for it. God loves you no matter what. His love for you does not have anything to do with you walking in holiness and obedience. Christ declares *"But now you must be holy in everything you do, just as God – who chose you to be his children-is holy. For he himself has said, you must be holy because I am holy"* (1Peter 1:15-16, NLT).

CHAPTER TWELVE

God Answers Our Prayers

He Hears What We Say When We Pray

I was praying in my car as I was driving to the beauty shop. I prayed in tongues for a while; I praised God for a while and then I started praying in the understanding (English). As I was talking to God, I asked Him to remember me and my husband past generosity to his people and to his church. I started naming some of the things we have done to help his church and his people over the years. As I was naming some of the things we have done, I paused and told God, even though our good works are like filthy rags, please bless us. **"And the Holy Ghost said, 'You are using the scripture wrong', "I said, 'I am?' The Holy Ghost said, "Yes, because I love the works you and Robert do; they are not filthy rags.'** The scripture that I was referring to was, *"We are all infected and impure with sin. When we proudly display our righteous deeds, we find they are but filthy rags"*(Isaiah 64:6, NLT). Today and even people in Bible days believed that their good works would get them into heaven. But that is not so. My prayer was not talking about trying to get into heaven with my good deeds. I was using the scripture to say that the works I do for Him was not good enough, because I am not perfect. "But the Holy Ghost corrected me and said, 'that the works that we had done were great in his sight.' God knew what I was trying to say in my prayers and he knew my heart. But the Holy Spirit corrected me, because the scripture was used incorrectly. This scripture means that your good (works) deeds are nothing to God if you think that they will get you into heaven. In other words, if you take your good works and try to use them to get you into heaven then they are filthy rags. God loves our good works when we are a blessing to his people and church with our time, money, and prayers. To sum it up, as we operate in the Fruit of the Spirit (Galatians 5:22) toward others then Jehovah God is pleased with us. Now I already knew that; but, I was still using the scripture wrong. And the Holy Ghost reminded me that I was using this scripture out of context. The only things that will get people into heaven is to believe in Christ. *"We are made right with God when we believe that Jesus shed his blood, sacrificing his life for us"(Romans 3:25, NLT). "For if you confess with our mouth that Jesus is Lord and believe in your heart that God raised him from the dead, you will be saved. For it is by believing in your heart that you are made right with God, and it is by confessing with your mouth that you are saved"(Roman 10:9-10, NLT).* When I used the scripture, Isaiah 64:6, I was not justifying my works to be good enough to enter heaven; but, I was saying that they were not good enough to please God. I was using the scripture out of context; because, I was identifying my good works with the wrong scripture. "God said, 'that our good deeds are great in his sight.' Praise the Lord! I believe on the cross and I have salvation and I know that this is the only way I will get into heaven. The Holy Ghost reminded me that our good works are accepted and that He loves them and that He knew that I was not trying to use my good work to enter heaven.

When we pray, God hears our prayer and He hears what we pray. Paul teaches us in Philippians that, we should pray with supplication. *"Be careful for nothing; but in everything by prayer and supplication with thanksgiving let your requests be made known unto God"* (Philippians 4:6, KJV). Supplication means to appeal to someone who has the power to grant the request. And that someone is Jehovah God. When we pray, we should back up our prayers with scripture. We should back up our request with the promises of God. We should pray the word of God. Whenever I pray, I always have a scripture for what I am asking God for. For example, when I pray for a financial blessing I pray *"The Lord will send rain at the proper time from his rich treasury in the heavens to bless all the works I do. You will lend to many nations, but you will never need to borrow from them" (Deuteronomy 28:12, NLT).* I declare that I will lend to nations and will not borrow. When I pray for a daily need to be met, I pray, *"And the same God who takes care of me will supply all your needs from his glorious riches, which have been given to us in Christ Jesus" (Philippians 4:19, NLT).* And then I declare that God is supplying all my needs right now; that my mortgage is paid, my utility bill is paid, and my automobile payment is paid in the name of Jesus. When I need healing I say, *"And Jesus went forth, and saw a great multitude, and was moved with compassion toward them, and he healed their sick"(Matthew 14:14, KJV).* Then I will say, 'Father the word said that you had compassion on the people and healed all their diseases. I declare that my body is being healed right now in the name of Jesus. After each prayer, we should always say in the name of Jesus, because Jesus said ask using my name and you shall have what you ask for. Jesus said, *"You can ask anything in my name, and I will do it, because the work of the Son brings glory to the Father. Yes, ask anything in my name and I will do it" (John 14:13-14, NLT).* Jesus also said you can ask the Father for something using my name and you shall have it. *"You didn't choose me. I chose you. I appointed you to go and produce fruit that will last, so that the Father will give you whatever you ask for, using my name"(John:15:16, NLT).* You can ask the Father, in Jesus name, and you shall have what you ask for. But, **remember when we pray we have to use the scripture in the right context.** If we do not, then we cancel out what we pray. The right scripture backs up what we are asking for. We are reminding God of what He said He will do in the Bible. **We are reminding God of his promises that He has made to us to bless us.**

God remembered David and made him king of Israel at the age of thirty; after He anointed him king as a child (1 Samuel 16:13, 2 Samuel 5:3-4). God remembered Hannah and blessed her with a child named Samuel (1 Samuel 1:19-20). God remembered the Israelites and delivered them out of seventy years of captivity (2 Chronicles 36:22-23). God remembered Samson and gave him one last victory over the Philistines (Judges 16:28-30). God remembered King Hezekiah and let him live another fifteen years (Isaiah 38:3-5). God remembered Rachel and gave her a son, Joseph (Genesis 30: 22). There are so many examples in the Bible of how God remembered his people and blessed them. God will remember your past deeds and bless you, too. Use the scripture correctly and in the right context when praying and asking God for something. You want your prayer to be a blessing to you. The Holy Spirit corrected me so that my prayers will be answered and not be a hindrance to me. **God loves us so much that He sees to it that we ask correctly when we need something from him**. This tells me that He hears me when I pray and that I will receive what I ask for. *"And we can be confident that he will listen to us whenever we ask him for anything in line with his will. And if we know he is listening when we make our request, we can be sure that he will give us what we ask for"(1 John 5:14-15, NLT)*. When you pray, align your scriptures correctly with what you are asking for because God wants to bless us and He wants us to be a blessing to his people. In this you will bring God much glory!

CHAPTER THIRTEEN

God Did Answer Your Prayer

But in His own Way

Did you hear from God? Did God answer your prayers? Yes, God has answered our prayers and we were not listening to him. When we think that God has not answered us, we keep on praying about the same situation. Or, we call on others to prayer for us or with us. You don't need anyone else to pray for you and you don't need a prayer partner; you need to listen for God's voice. He is speaking to you about your situation and He has given you the answer to your question. He is talking to you. He has answered your prayer for help and He is answering you now. He might have sent the answer through a friend, family or your pastor. He might have sent your answer through the Bible. You may have received your answer when you were driving in your car and listening to the radio or when you read something on a bill board. What was written on the bill board might be your answer. He may have given you a vision or a dream. Someone might have prophesied your answer to you or God might have spoken to you personally. He might be talking to you now and you're just ignoring him and not listening. God could have told you the answer ten years ago and you have forgotten about it. God always answers. *"I will answer them before they even call to me. While they are still talking to me about their needs, I will go ahead and answer their prayers"* *(Isaiah 65:24, NLT).*

The book of Ephesians says that all of our blessings are located in the spiritual realm. These blessings are the answer to your prayers. *"All praise to God, the Father of our Lord Jesus Christ, who has blessed us with every spiritual blessing in the heavenly realms because we are united with Christ" Ephesian:1:3, NLT)*. **Every answer that we are looking for to our prayers is located in the spiritual realm.** God has sent the answer; but, He might not have sent the answer in the way we were looking for it to come. But, He does answer. The word says that God does things in mysterious ways. *"Truly, O God of Israel, our Savior, you work in strange and mysterious ways"(Isaiah 45:15, NLT)*. Since we know God works in strange ways, we should try to listen for his voice. We are not listening or we just can't hear him. **It could be that our hearing is clouded from the worries of this world.** In the book of Matthew Jesus says, blessed are your eyes that see and your ears hear. But so many people see and hear and don't understand. Jesus said, *"You will hear my words, but you will not understand; you will see what I do, but you will not perceive its meaning" (Matthew 13:14, NLT)*. Our lack of understanding of the way God does things and the cares of this world stop us from hearing, seeing and understanding what God is trying to do in our lives. Ask God to help you understand, accept and hear the answer He is giving you for your problems. My problem was that I had forgotten that He had already given me a word about my situation. So, when the situation arose, concerning my son I called on my prayer partners to pray and God rebuked me for it. **"The Holy Spirit said to me, 'why do you need prayer partners when I have already given you an answer about the situation concerning your son.'** I talk about this in my book "Faith That Works" chapter six titled "No More Prayer Partners". Things did not turn out like I thought they should concerning my son. And when that happened I said to myself, "God has not answered my prayer concerning my son and I need to pray more for him and I will get help from my prayer partners." But He did answer my prayer about my son and He gave me the answer long ago. I had just forgotten. Things weren't happening the way I thought they should, so I said that God had not sent the answer; but He did answer my prayer.

We have to remember that not only does God do things in mysterious ways; God thoughts and ways are different from ours. The Lord said this to Isaiah, *"My thoughts are completely different from yours, says the Lord. And my ways are far beyond anything you could imagine. For just as the heavens are higher than the earth, so are my ways higher than your ways and my thoughts higher than your thoughts"* (Isaiah 55:8-9, NLT). **When we look for God to send an answer He sends the opposite answer of what we expect.** Then it looks like He has not sent an answer for our problem, because the answer God sent was different from what you were looking for and from what you were thinking the answer should be. God's thoughts and ways are different from ours and when we don't understand what is happening we say that God has not answered our prayers; but, indeed He has. The answer that God gives might seem crazy, difficult or unreal. It might not feel right, it might not look right and we just don't like the answer. But that's your answer. God has gotten it right and He has sent the answer on time even though it does not look like the answer.

In the situation concerning my son, everything was taking place opposite of the way I thought it should. But, I did have an answer. It did not look like my answer, it did not feel like my answer, and I did not like the answer, but, it was the answer. I had to believe the way the situation was unfolding at the time was the answer to my problem. In the natural realm it did not look so good; but, God had already worked out everything in the spirit realm. My problem caused me lots of pain, hurt and anger. But I survived it any way. *"And we know that God causes everything the to work together for the good of those who love God and are called according to his purpose for them"* (Romans 8:28, NLT). When I look back on the situation everything did work out and I wouldn't have wanted it any other way. And I did not need to pray about it again, because He had given me the answer. **I just needed to believe that even though my answer did not look**

right, indeed it was the answer. Oh, you want to know what happened. Well, my son quit school, left home and moved in with his girlfriend and her family unmarried. He moved in with her family and slept on the couch. His girlfriend was not pregnant he just did not want to live with me and his daddy in our home. We felt betrayed. What had we done for him to hate us so much? He left the rich life that we had provided for him to move where he felt much freer and happier. We had too many strict rules for him. From there, he and his girlfriend left her parents house and moved into an apartment. This is the day I wrote, 'No More Prayer Partners' in my book Faith That Works because this was the day he came home to get his bed. What do you do in a situation when you know you have given and done all you can for your children and they don't turn out like you expect? You wonder where I went wrong. I am here to tell you that if you provide for your children to the best of your ability and they still go astray; you have not done anything wrong. So, stop blaming yourself. Remember there is a real devil and his job is to spread evil throughout the world. If Satan cannot get you, then he will try to get your children. But there is also a merciful God who not only loves you, but He loves your seeds and He will save your children. Your job is to believe that God is protecting your children and that he is working things out on your behalf. My son and his girlfriend lived together for almost two years before she got pregnant. This was not an accident; they planned the pregnancy. I found out later that my son always wanted to marry her, but would not until I gave them my blessing. I became so upset with the whole situation that at one time we did not know where our son worked or where he lived during those two years. I just prayed for protection and blessings on him. And God assured me many times that he was in his hands and that He was taking care of him. Many nights I cried and cried and cried for my child to come home. "And all I would say was 'God bring him home.' In my heart, I was saying bring my son back to my house to live. Bring my son home, Lord. Then one day he came to visit. Big Robert and I were in the bedroom and we heard the alarm beep letting us know that someone was coming into the house. When we got up to see who was coming into our house it was our son. I was so glad to see him. But, he had this serious look on his face. I want to talk to you was all he said. I asked if anything was wrong. He said no mom. Then he told us that his girlfriend was pregnant and that she would have the baby in about six weeks. To say the least we were not happy and I was very upset with him. How could he get this girl pregnant? Again, those thoughts of where we went wrong came. Why is this happening to us? We're good parents. He was not even married. I wondered why he hadn't married her yet? Later, when I was in prayer God revealed to me that the only reason that he was not married was because of me. God told me that he was waiting for me to tell him that is was fine to marry her. A couple of weeks after the initial shock, I finally called Little Robert into my office. I asked him 'is this my grandbaby.' "He said, 'Yes mommy.' I said, 'if this is my grandbaby then you can't bring my grandbaby here without our name; you must marry her.' I have never seen him so happy. I had not seen a smile so big on his face since he was a child. It was like his whole world had come back together. By the next weekend he was married. And the next month they had a baby boy. And when we saw that boy through the hospital window, he looked just like me. God always has a sense of humor. Who else could have made the baby come out looking just like the grandmother, but God? When I look at him now, I see me. The way he acts and the things he does are just what my son did as a child. There is no denying that God had his hand in this. Everything worked out the way God wanted it to work out and God got the glory for this. Later, God revealed to us that He has called our grandson to preach his word. Jeremiah says, "*For I know the plans I have for you says the Lord. They are plans for good and not for disaster, to give you a future and a hope*" (*Jeremiah 29:11, NLT*). We did not know this all would turn out so great and God would get the glory. God did have a plan; but, we did not see it.

God has a plan for you and your family. Don't be taken aback when the answer doesn't look favorable. Just believe that God is working out all problems on your behalf and that if you let him you will get the victory in the end. So, my son did come back home, but not to physically live there. He came back home to us in his heart. And guess what my son came back with a loving grandson. God sent my son back to us with a family. Hallelujah!

CHAPTER FOURTEEN

I Can't Tell It, but God Knows

God Knows

I am now in a bind and I can't tell anyone about it. I could lose everything in a matter of weeks. All odds are against me and the only person I can turn to is God. I don't have anyone that I can talk to or confide my deepest secrets to. Everyone depends on me, how can I tell them that I don't have enough faith? Or that I am tired of waiting and I wonder when God will show up to rescue me from my despair? I can't tell anyone what's really bothering me; it will show my lack of faith. I am the faith woman. I am not supposed to get depressed or have no faith. Who will understand? Who will pray with me or for me? I'm supposed to be strong and full of courage. No fear should be on me. I am a woman of God. I encourage other people; I don't get discouraged. I help people and no one helps me. I'm ashamed because I need help and I have no patience to wait upon the Lord. How did I get into this trouble? What happened? Will I ever be able to recover? What will others think? They will say, "There goes the one that calls on the Lord; she has so much faith and her God has not rescued her." *"O Lord, I have so many enemies, so many are against me. So many are saying, God will never rescue him"* (Psalms 3:1-2, NLT). Look at her. She's nothing; she claims that God will supply all her needs. That's what she tells us. So where is her God when she needs him? She tells us don't worry cast all your worries upon him. Look she's not only worrying, but she is in fear. She says no weapon formed against you will prosper. But look at her, all odds are against her. Her enemy has won, they have conquered her. She can't even fight back. Yes, she is too weak and stressed out to fight. She keeps on praying but to no avail. Her prayers are weak. She is at a loss of words to pray. She tries to pray in tongues. She tries to put on the full Armor of God. But she gets no answer from her mighty God. Who will rescue her in her time of need? She has nowhere to turn. In her own house her husband is depressed. He can't offer her rest and they look at each other in despair. Hopelessness, all is gone they say. They are so depressed that they can't even encourage each other. Who will save them? They don't fight among themselves anymore. They go around quiet as though someone will come to capture them if they make too much noise. They speak nice to each other. For some reason this bad situation has brought them closer together. They try to comfort each other the best way they can with soft spoken words. But where did their boldness go? Where did the confidence they had in their Father go? Where did all that courage go? And where is their faith?

It all disappeared in a moment. Did it happen when trouble first struck or did it happen over a period of time or as Satan kept throwing those fiery darts? One trial, one tribulation, and one test after another. Did all those trials wear them down? Or, were they just faking it about their faith. They have been beaten up so badly by the thoughts in their minds. It's so disturbing. They think on what will happen to them if things do not change and if God doesn't come soon. This makes them feel discouraged and sad. They forgot that none of those things have ever happened. But they keep saying, if God doesn't come now! What will we do? They just want to go and hide. They'd rather dig a hole and hide in it from the world and all of its troubles. They said trouble is everywhere and we just can't get out. The enemy is in the shadows waiting for the right time to take them out. They pray that God will cover them with his wings and shelter them from all harm. They cry out to God where is my protection that you promised? When will you come and deliver us from all this destruction? Will it be today or will we have to wait another day? I can't go on another day or I'll die if I have to go through this again. Where is your God why don't you answer? I can't hear you. Come to my rescue. You said those who have heavy burdens you will give them rest. You said come to my throne room and we can receive mercy and grace in our time of need. We have been to the throne room, but we did find any answers. We look for God, but we don't see him. We call on his name and he did not answer. But wait, did he answer me in his still small voice. Did he send a message through a friend or a dream that we just ignored? Did he really answer? Or has he told us long ago the answer to our problems that we are having now? You keep on praying waiting to hear from the Father. Sure, a Father answers his children.

So I picked myself up and said I will rejoice, because the word said we should rejoice in all things. *"Always be joyful. Keep on praying. No matter what happens, always be thankful, for this is God's will for you who belong to Christ Jesus (1 Thessalonians 5:16-18, NLT).* But it is still another day without an answer. I drive to the beauty shop; I pray and ask God for help. As I pray and cry out to him to save us, **"I hear a still small voice saying 'Be still and know that I am God.'** Be still and know that I am God. Yes, I know that God is all powerful, that he is faithful, that he is a delivering God and that he loves me. I know that God can deliver me in my time of need. But do I really believe these words or was I just speaking them? Did I really believe that God will do it for me and did I have the courage and patience to wait upon him? "I said to myself, 'where my heart is and where my mind is?' Do I really believe? The test of time will tell. Was I just going through the motions or do I really believe that God will deliver me? Did I really have strong faith or just claiming to have faith? This test will tell what I am really made of? Did I believe all those things about faith that I wrote in my book and told people? Now my faith was being put to the test and what will I do? "I said God, 'you are not speaking to me and telling me what to do. You aren't giving me the direction I so badly need. You have not told me what the outcome will be. I have not heard from you. You are silent.' **Have you ever felt like you're waiting for God to say something or do something and He says or does nothing?** I had been waiting for weeks to hear from him and for God to do something; like destroy my enemies. But I heard nothing and nothing changed. But on the way to the beauty shop, **"He said, 'Be still and know that I am God.' "Then he said, 'I've been talking to you all the time. You have not been tuning in.' "He said, 'When you were standing at your dresser, I told you all is well.' "You said, 'Sure all is well, but not for me. You spoke and then you thought. You spoke sure all is well, but you thought not for me. Then I confirmed what I was telling you by letting one of your friend call you, the first thing, "she said was, 'All is well Brenda.' You just smiled and thought that's what you say God all is well.** Now all is well comes from 2 Kings 4. God gave me those word years ago when he told me that although everything was dying the Shunammite women kept declaring, all is well. God can take what is dead and bring it back to life."**Then God said, 'Your friend said in her conversation just before you received a big blessing everything falls apart. That was a word for you. I gave you a word. Then I sent another word through your husband dream.'** In my husband dream, a tornado was coming toward him and the children. And when the tornado got close to him; it went past him and over his head not touching the children, building or him. When he told you the dream you gave him the interpretation which was that you are under attack and even though the attack hit close to home nothing will be destroyed, because it will just pass right by us. God also reminded me of another time, **"He had spoken to me saying, 'Then one night when you were in prayer I told you several times no weapon formed against you will prosper. I told you that so many times that night until you asked me Father, why do you keep saying that?" "And I said, 'just remember that no weapon formed against you shall prosper.'** I thought on these things and God had indeed answered me. *"What can we say about such wonderful things as these? If God is for us, who can ever be against us"(Romans 8:31, NLT).* He was not silent. I just was not paying attention.

But I was still weak in my ability to move forward and break out of this depression. I asked God to help me in my faith, to help me be strong, and to help me to overcome my fears. **"And he said for me to say over and over again, 'No weapon formed against me will prosper.'** In other words, tribulation will come, but it will never overcome us. We will get the victory in the end. When I put all these things together I had an answer from God. God was with me. He told me that He would fight our battle and we were going to win.

One day our yard man came and said, "Brenda, pray for me because the last time you prayed that sickness off me, I was healed. "So, I prayed for him and for myself. After praying for him, I thought, I have faith for you to get what you need from God, but do I have enough faith to get what I need from him? God brought back to my attention a prayer that I prayed ten days earlier for $3,800. I was in my office and I said, "God, I need $3,800." And that is all I said and went on. A friend called me the same morning and said God had been trying to get her up around 3:00 am in the morning for two nights, so she finally got up last night and the number 3800.00 came to her. She felt it in her heart and said to herself, "I must need to send Brenda 3800.00 for her mortgage." She called me and asked me what my mortgage was, but found out that its double that amount. So, she was a little confused, but she still felt that the Lord told her to send me 3800.00 and maybe it was for something else. She had $3800.00 put into my account. God answered a simple prayer of faith, something that I had forgotten about. **"God told me that, 'I do have faith. I have the kind of faith that speaks and forget that I asked.'** **"And God said, 'I did not forget what you asked me for. I have the kind of faith when I speak something and forget it; it is because I figure it is already done.'**

No use in crying over spilled milk, I ask and I expect to receive. I not only do that for me, but for everyone I pray for. I expected

God to do something. I know He will do something. My problem is **waiting**. I want him to do something now, and if He isn't going to do it now I want to know when. So when I got depressed it was not because I did not believe God would answer my prayer. I wanted to know when God would do it. How long did I have to wait? What I needed to improve on while waiting? And why I have to wait so long? Hurry Up Lord! I said. Please Hurry up. I will die out here. **"But God just says, 'patience; be still, wait upon me.'**

Well, in all my worrying, impatience, and stress, I still can't manage to make God move in a hurry. God is working with me on this. Because He always tells me that He is not on my time and that He can change my circumstances before I can blink my eye. *"But if we look forward to something we don't have yet, we must wait patiently and confidently"* ((Romans 8:25, NLT). God doesn't have to answer you when you think He should. He will perform a miracle in your life you just need to know that He will. God will answer and He will answer on time. He has a miracle for you now. This is my secret that I could not tell, my deepest thoughts that could ruin me and hurt someone else that depended on me. Someone else might have thought that I had a lack of faith. I don't have a lack of faith, but a lack of patience. For the word says, *"God has made everything beautiful for its own time"(Ecclesiastes 3:11NLT).*

CHAPTER FIFTEEN

Are you Being Attacked for No Reason at All

Under Attack who Cares

You are just minding your own business and bad things start to happen to you. You are not bothering anyone; you are just trying to live a good life. But, one disaster after another keeps happening to you. You get sick; you did not ask for sickness but you just got sick. It might be a cold or a chronic disease. One day you get sick and the doctor says you have cancer; you did not ask for cancer. As a matter of fact, you have been taking good care of yourself so why did you get cancer? You get a cold. You did not ask for a cold. Where did it come from? You feel miserable. Did it come from your children or were you in a public place and you picked up a virus? What happened? You're driving to work and you did not plan to have a wreck. But a car came out of nowhere and hit you. Your insurance is cancelled; because, it elapsed for some reason or another. It might be because you did not get the bill in the mail and it did not get paid or you took the money to pay something else more important. You go to work today and you get fired and you did not see it coming. You just received your evaluation from your employer and it was good. But you were still fired. He said, we have to cut back. What can you do? Your husband or wife comes home one day and say I'm leaving; I don't want to be married anymore. You know you have been having some problems, but you did not think it would lead to this. Or you didn't have any problems and your marriage was great. But the other person just doesn't want to be married to you anymore. What's up with this? Your appliances just stop working for no apparent reason at all. They are not old, but you don't have a warranty. Someone dies in your family or a friend dies and they were not even sick. Then you raise your hands in the air saying, What's Wrong! Someone accuses you of something you know nothing about and people are gossiping about you. You didn't do anything to these people. But you are the gossip of the town and they accuse you of things you know nothing about. You say, why try to please people? Or why have friends, because it's just like being friends with an enemy. You wake up in the morning and you are depressed for no reason at all. You think all odds are against you. That is Satan at work against you. He attacks you in your mind. Telling you nothing is going to work out for you leaving you feeling defeated, hopeless and depressed. You can't break that cycle so you stay depressed for days; sometimes years. You did not ask for that, but it happens and it happens to you. You say why so many problem? Why so much stress? You don't know why, but it all happens and you are trying to endure each situation.

Now let's look at what the book of Ecclesiastes says. Solomon says that everything is meaningless. And we should spend our time loving and knowing God. Solomon says, *"So now I hate life because everything done here under the sun is so irrational. Everything is meaningless, like chasing the wind" (Ecclesiastes 2:17, NLT).* Is this true? Everything is futile. Everything is unpredictable. Everything is meaningless. Is it like going in circles? Over and over again bad things happen to us. Is it just like the scripture says we are under attack and our bodies are being destroyed daily. We know that Satan is trying to destroy us. The Bible tells us that Satan aimed his fiery darts at us. One dart after another before one problem is solved another one comes. The book of Ephesians says that the power of God through prayer, faith, the word of God, salvation, peace, righteousness, and truth destroy the works of Satan. Yes, putting on the full Armor of God destroys the works of the devil. **So, don't be surprised that you are going through something, put on God's armor and fight.** *"Dear friends, don't be surprised at the fiery trials you are going through, as if something strange were happening to you" (1Peter 4:12, NLT).* You say to yourself, strange. Why do I serve a good and all powerful God? I am not supposed to have these trials. But, that is not true. The same trials that you are having is not only happening to you but to everybody. *"Remember that your Christian brothers and sisters all over the world are going through the same kind of suffering you are" (1Peter5:9, NLT).* You are not the only one suffering; but, can you survive.

Can you stand strong and endure the many trials that you face? God calls these trials tests. Can you endure your tests, because you will have plenty of them? For what Satan meant to hurt you with, God turns it into a test for you. All bad things come from Satan trying to stop you from receiving God's best in your life. Even though we have to endure these trials, **God warns you of your troubles and He helps you through them.** That is why the scriptures say, *"Be careful! Watch out for attacks from the Devil, your great enemy. He prowls around like a roaring lion, looking for some victim to devour"(1Peter 5:8, NLT).* That is why we must be aware of what Satan is trying to do to us so that we stand strong in faith with prayer. We stand strong when we are under attack. Remember we are not fighting against flesh and blood, but we are fighting against the wiles and schemes of the deceiver, Satan himself.

So there will be times of suffering, but if we suffer we will also share in the reward that God gives to his servants that refuse to quit or give up. *"And since we are his children, we will share his treasure for everything God gives to his Son, Christ is ours, too. But if we are to share his glory, we must also share his suffering"(Romans 8:17, NLT).* When we belong to God we must carry our cross too. We will suffer just as Christ did. But if we refuse to quit, we will receive a reward just like Christ did. Therefore, we have to hold on and endure our problems or our tests until our blessings come. There will be times of tribulation.

A friend called me from Atlanta and said, "Brenda I went on my daily four mile walk this morning and I had an accident. She said, "I just fell". She broke her front tooth, bruised her face and her lip was swollen. She goes on to say, "It look like I've gotten beat up. I did not trip and nothing was in front of me, and that this is the same route I take every day. I felt a push in my back and before I knew it I had fallen and landed on my face, then I felt another push from behind my head pushing my face into the concrete". I thought to myself what is going on? She did not ask to fall; she had no intention on falling and hurting herself. So what happened? Then she gave me the answer when she said *"I was just praying in tongues.* As I was praying in tongues God the Holy Spirit came upon me and God had laid a prayer on my heart to pray out aloud. So, I started speaking that prayer out and the next thing I knew I was on the ground". What happened? My friend had made Satan mad. **He knows when we have God's power he cannot stop us.**

Satan does not want us to have God's power, because he is defenseless against us when we do. The power of God overcomes Satan and his evil works and he is defeated. He does not want us to have victory. Satan knows he is defeated when Christ is working through us. The works of Satan were defeated at the cross. We need to know that and believe it because we are under attack from Satan himself. Things are happening around you every day that does not make sense. Satan will make you think that no one else is having these problems but you. Now, that's a good laugh. That's what you think? Everyone is having the same problem that you have and probably more than you. **That is why you must know God and serve him with your whole heart.**

When we know God and serve him, He fights our battles. He takes the tribulations that we go through and turn them into a test. This test is to benefit us. *"And we know that God causes everything to work together for the good of those who love God and are called according to his purpose for them"(Romans 8:28, NLT).* God takes what the devil meant to harm you and works it to your benefit in the form of a test. God loves you and you love him and He pours his grace upon you in times of troubles; for He will help you. So, get to know God with your whole heart because you will not survive without him. You can always depend on him to get you through all your tough times. This is the key to our troubles whatever they may be. We need the power of God. And we do this by loving and knowing him. My friend did not stop walking; she kept on going she said, "I had another two miles to go." She got up with her mouth bleeding and kept up what she was doing. She did not let that stop her. She said she kept on praying in tongues and speaking out the prayer that God had given her. She also said that she always prays that God will protect her when she walks and that He promised her protection. **She had a word from God.** She did not quit or turn around she kept on going. My friend stood on the word that God had given her. **She was afflicted, but not defeated. Yes, she was bruised and hurting but that still did not deter her, she kept on going. We should never let Satan's attack keep us from accomplishing what God has told us to do.** In other words, we should never let evil stop us from reaching our goal. She had not reached her goal and she was not going to turn around. My friend was determined to get to the finish line. This is how we must be when problems arise in our life. We must keep on pushing until we reach our goal. Luke 18:1 says *"Men ought to pray and never give up"*. Things might seen unpredictable, unreasonable, uncomfortable, unreliable, unconventional, but never quit or go back. Keep on pushing through every obstacle, problem, bad situation, or disaster because if you do you are guaranteed a victory. You will win. God has not left you He is right beside you going through every affliction and enduring every pain with you. He will deliver you from all circumstances. *"So if you are suffering according to God's will, keep on doing what is right, and trust yourself to the God who made you, for he will never fail you"*(1 Peter 4:19, NLT). Just depend on and believe in him, He is not a liar and in due season you will reap if you faint not. So don't give up, but stay in faith. You will get the victory; you will reach your goals. And the

Lord shall deliver you, keeping your feet stable and secure in times of trouble. *"In that day he will be your sure foundation, providing a rich store of salvation, wisdom, and knowledge. The fear of the Lord is the key to this treasure"(Isaiah 33:6, NLT).*

So, let's take some advice from Solomon for he says who can enjoy anything apart from knowing God. In the end, God will judge Satan and his servants. We will be judged too, but for our good works. We should work hard at knowing and loving God; because, without him we are nothing. Without God, everything we do is meaningless. And remember what Peter said, *"In his kindness God called you to his eternal glory by means of Jesus Christ. After you have suffered a little while, He will restore, support, and strengthen you, and He will place you on a firm foundation"(1Peter 5:10, NLT).* Yes, in due season you will be blessed, you will not fail and you will be stronger than ever. In that day God himself will make you stable and secure and set you in a place of abundance.

CHAPTER SIXTEEN

The Enemy Is Close By

Don't Let the Enemy Get You Down

Do you have an enemy close by you? I'm talking about an enemy that is right in your household living with you. It might be your husband, children, parents, relatives or friends. They are there, watching your every move. They are waiting for you to fall so that they can say I told you so. I told you that you would not make it. I told you that it would not happen for you. I told you that God would not deliver you.

They make smart remarks about everything you do. They ask all kind of questions, why do you do this? Or why do you do that? **They themselves are wishing for a better life, but they are not willing to take the risk. However, they get angry at you when you take the risk.** When you spend time in prayer, they ask why you pray all the time. When you fast, they ask why you fast, nothing is going to change. They sneer at all you do for the Lord. In their heart they are hoping that their opinion is wrong. **But they just can't come to the realization that God will work for you and for them. They find it safer to stay in disbelief for fear of getting hurt if they start believing.** So they make your life miserable, because you choose to believe without reservation. They hope that God will come and deliver you, so they can believe that God might remember them and do something for them too. But, are they willing to stick their necks out and take a chance? Instead of just keeping quiet, they attack you for believing and confessing your faith in the Lord. They attack you for moving forward on what the Lord has told you to do. They are afraid to move forward and more afraid to believe that God will do something good for them. They have been waiting a long time for God to answer their prayers and you have been waiting a long time for God to answer your prayers also. But you have a better attitude than they have; because, you have not lost hope. They have in some cases lost hope; they are bitter, tired and disappointed in themselves and God. Yes, they are disappointed in God for not showing up and meeting their needs. They blame God and you for their circumstance. They do not take credit for anything that has gone wrong in their life. It is always easier to blame someone else. You get blamed because you have not lost hope, you have not become bitter and you still believe that God is on his way to restore you. **You remain positive in the midst of your affliction.** They cannot see the future so they believe what they hear, they believe what they feel and they believe what they see.

On the other hand you believe God and in the midst of your affliction God sustains you. This gets them on edge and angry at you. They will not believe in God's miracle working power. They get angry at you because you believe during hard times, and they don't see how you can still believe God while going through all the tribulations. They are in fear and running. You are standing in faith and you refuse to run. They don't realize that you are hurting too. They are hurting you more by the constant attacks on you. But God sees all your affliction and He will deliver you and shut the lion's mouth. God will show up and show up strong. He will make man out to be a liar and His words to be true. In the end it will all be worth it. **Don't let the haters get you down, but continue to STAND.** *"I wash my hands to declare my innocence. I come to your altar, O Lord, singing a song of thanksgiving and telling of all your miracles" (Psalm 26: 6-7, NLT).*

CHAPTER SEVENTEEN

Satan is Rich

Let's Take His Stuff!

I have never heard any one speak on this subject. The devil is rich, let's take his stuff. You always hear how the devil is taking our stuff. Well, the devil has plenty of stuff so let's take his stuff from him. I use to ask the Lord why evil people prosper. I would hear other preachers saying we live in an evil world and evil people prosper. We hear that God keeps on blessing them, giving them a chance to repent. We see this in Genesis 15:16, when God is talking to Abraham about blessing him and his generation with great wealth after four hundred years. God was waiting for the sins of the Amorites to run its course. They were living in the land when God gave Abraham the promise. During this time, God in his mercy was giving the Amorites time to repent and turn to him. Even though He knew that they would never repent and receive him as their Lord. Also, these people were a blessed people even though they did not serve God. Even today, there are so many people from all walks of life that do not serve God and they are blessed. This leads me to think that the devil has blessings also for his people. But remember God still blesses those who do not serve him, because of his mercy. But this too will end at a set time and they will be punished if they do not repent. Since the Amorites did not repent and turn to God they were destroyed and lost their land to the Israelites. We see that God does bless evil people, but if they do not turn from their sins and repent they will be punished.

The devil is fully equipped to bless his people. When Jesus was in the wildness the devil offered him the kingdom of the world if Jesus would bow down and worship him. *"Next the devil took him to the peak of a very high mountain and showed him the nations of the world and all their glory. I will give it all to you he said if you will only kneel down and worship me" (Matthew 4:8-9, NLT).* We see the devil owns the nation of the world and all their glory, so he is fully equipped to bless. I had never heard that until the Holy Spirit put in my mind that the devil has blessings. Then I said, 'well if he has blessings then we need to take them from him. Instead of only taking back what he stole from us let's go and take the devils stuff.' I made up in my mind then that the devil would not steal from me again and that I was going to steal from him because God wants me to have it. I told God, 'the devil is not going to do anything good with all that stuff, so I will make a plan and put forth the effort to get all I can from him.' **I never heard anyone say that the devil is fully equipped to bless his people. The devil blesses his people to do his works. Just like God blesses his people to do God's work.**

The devil blesses his people to spread evil and to influence people to live for him. God blesses his people to spread the gospel and to live for him. But, don't forget what I said earlier, occasionally, God does bless evil people so that they will see God's goodness and return or come to him for salvation.' So we are not talking about those people. We are talking about the devil and his personal servants that live, love and serve only him and do not have plans on changing sides. This is what you get when you serve the devil. When you have the blessings of the devil you don't have peace, you worry about getting caught in your evil, you risk going to jail, you worry about losing all that you have, you don't have divine health, you might be an alcoholic or a drug addict, and you might be depressed or oppressed, your family and relationships are dysfunctional, your life is a total mess. You might have the devil's blessings of money, big homes, beautiful automobiles, and all the material possessions, but you live in misery, fear, and fear of going to hell. Remember even though the devil blesses you, he is the one that comes to steal, kill, and destroy. *"The devil comes to kill, steal, and destroy"(John 10:10, NLT)*. You might be blessed by what the devil gives you, but you are dying and you are being destroyed daily. The word says that God rain on the just and unjust. Some of the turmoil that happens to the devil's servant happens also to God's servant. The different is that when you are God's servant, when bad things happen you have peace, hope and God is always with you bringing you out in victory. When God blesses you, you have life and life more abundantly. *"God comes to give life and life more abundantly" (John 10:10, NLT)*. Not only do you have God's blessing you have God's life, not death. And the word of scripture says remain in me and I in you so that you can produce much fruit. *"Yes, I am the vine you are the branches. Those who remain in me, and I in them, will produce much fruit. Those apart from me you can do nothing" (John15:5, NLT)*. I say all this to help you understand that the devil has blessings that we want and can get from him. Nice automobiles, finances, large homes and many material possessions. We should live great, healthy, and prosperous lives not the person that is serving the devil. Since we know that the devil possesses these things, let's take them from him.

Before I move on let's clean up a wrong thought. People might think that the house, automobile, money, and material possessions are evil, but you need to remember that things are not evil. It is what you do with these things. God told the Israelites this, *"The Lord will give you an abundance of good things in the land he swore to give your ancestors many children, numerous livestock, and abundant crops" (Deuteronomy 28:11, NLT)*. God promised to give us these things so there is nothing wrong with material possessions; it's what you do with them. A good example is when the FBI invades and takes possessions of personal property from people; they have an auction and sell all that was confiscated. The items they take possession of are clothing, jewelry, homes, automobiles and plenty of money. Everything is expensive and beautiful. Most of the time, these people do not know or serve God. The FBI takes the money that they acquire and use it to start new programs within the FBI offices. The items they confiscate are not evil. They are sold in auctions to the world. These items can be sold to a person that loves and serves God. These items will be a blessing to them and others. It is what you do with these things, not the things themselves. Items are not evil, people are. Now with that in mind let's focus on how we will take what belongs to the devil and use it for God's Kingdom.

We will not take what belongs to the devil by serving him, but by being just the opposite. We will take what the devil has by the word of God. We find in the scriptures that it pleases God in every way when we start focusing on taking things from the devil. We don't do anything evil that would please the devil; but, we will do what is pleasing to God. Remember, people who serve the devil are cursed and those that serve the living God have life. Moses tells us this in his third address to the Israelites. Moses says, *"Now listen. Today I am giving you a choice between prosperity and disaster, between life and death. I have commanded you today to love your God and to keep his commands, laws and regulation by walking in his ways"* (Deuteronomy 30:15-16, NLT). Then Moses goes on to tell the people, *"Today I have given you the choice between life and death, between blessings and curses. I call on heaven and earth to witness the choice you make. Oh, that you would choose life, that you and your descendants might live"*(Deuteronomy 30:19, NLT). If you love the Lord then you will obey his commandants; but if you don't love him how can you obey him.

When you serve the devil you will die. You can only have life by serving God. We must have a renewed mind. Your mind must change to walk in righteousness. *"Don't copy the behavior and customs of this world, but let God transform you into a new person by changing the way you think. Then you will know what God wants you to do, and you will know how good and pleasing and perfect his will really is"* (Romans12:3, NLT). When you make a choice to serve God, you will renew your mind by the word of God, and then you will be able to take what the devil has **When we serve God with our whole heart then we are taking back from this world what the devil says is his.** He does not have control over us to take from us, instead we take from him. We are full of faith and our minds and hearts are focused on Jesus. Remember, the word says, 'Satan is the present usurper of this world's system. But when we follow Jesus with a pure heart and pure motives we can always have the best.' **Every time we obey the scripture, keep our faith, love others, and walk in the Fruit of the Spirit we are pleasing God.** Every time we do this we are taking something from the devil. Every time we do good things we will receive good. And when we receive these blessings they will not be curses. God reverses the curses from possessions, because we love and serve him. We can have our piece of the pie. We can have our own worldly possessions, and use them to spread the gospel to the world. Not only will we be a blessing to others, but we too will be blessed. But on the other hand, if you don't love God and keep his commandants then you are receiving your blessings from the devil and whatever you receive from him will be cursed and death will follow. So I say to you today, choose life that you may receive your full inheritance from the Lord and be blessed.

CHAPTER EIGHTEEN

Waiting For A Miracle

God Way

Have you ever waited for something a long time? Have you waited on God to do a miracle? Are you expecting a miracle or the answer to your prayers? Well, I found myself waiting on God to do a miracle in my life instead of waiting on the answer to my prayers? I realized that this was the wrong thing to do. Let me explain what I am talking about. My husband needed healing badly and we found that instead of waiting for the healing, we were waiting for a miracle. In 2004 we thought that God had healed his back but his back was not healed. He only received relief for the pain he had in his back for a while. Then pain came back and he needed to be healed in his body. He needed back surgery to receive his healing. If he had moved forward and had not waited for a miracle then Robert could of being heal long ago. He would have received healing in his body for his back and had no more pain. We weren't waiting for God to answer to our prayers; we were waiting for a miracle so we did not get the surgery. So for many years, he suffered unnecessarily. He could have been healed a long time ago with the surgery. Now, I find myself at 5:30 am in the morning waiting for him to come out of a five hour and thirty minute surgery. All these years we have been waiting for God to miraculously heal his body. God always said that He would heal my husband and He wants to heal him. We knew

God wanted to heal him, but instead of us inquiring about how God wanted to heal him, we expected God to heal him miraculously. It never happened. It never occurred to us that God wanted to send Robert's healing through surgery and medication. We had said to ourselves "we know God can heal through medicine but we want a miracle. We have enough faith to believe for a miracle" and this is where we went wrong. We did not give God a chance to do what He wanted to do. We did not give God a chance to manifest his blessing in Robert's life. We had already decided that we wanted a miraculous healing from God and that we would wait on God for that miraculous healing; and that is what we did and during that long wait he suffered. If we had just considered that God wanted to heal him through medicine and not the way we thought or wanted him to be healed, God would have healed him.

We as faith Christians miss the mark most to the time. We believe that God wants the best for us. We believe that God will take care of us and meet all of our needs. **But we try to orchestrate the way God will do his job.** When we ask God for something we should expect him to answer. **Our job is to expect God to answer not to tell him how to answer our prayers. We should not put demands on the way He wants to send the blessing. When we put those demands on God we limit the blessings of the Lord in our life.** When we already have the answer, and we already know how we want God to bless us then we stop the manifestation of God's blessing in our lives. God wants to send the blessing his way, not ours. When He does send the blessing we refuse the way He sends it because we expected it to come in a different way. This is what happened to us. Robert could have been healed with surgery years ago when I wrote a book entitled 'Healing Is for You'. In the book, I wrote a chapter about God healing Robert's body. You see, in the chapter, several people prayed for Robert's healing. And we thought that he was healed, but he was not. He got plenty of relief, but he did not become completely healed. No, he was not healed and no he did not lose his healing because of a lack of faith. The healing never did come; because, God had planned to heal Robert completely through surgery. God does work through medicine to heal. God can perform a miracle, but He will and almost always use medicine. I am in the waiting room now and, **"God is saying to me, 'That Robert could have been healed long ago. He would not have had to suffer for so long. This is what happens to my people when they get confused about what I am doing. They try to put me in a box and limit what I am trying to do for them. They want all the control. So they decide what kind of blessing they want, when they want the blessing, how the blessing should come to them and they reject all that I'm trying to do for them. They have their own idea and they want me to fix it in line with what they want. They forget what Jeremiah 23:8 said, "*I don't know the thoughts that you have toward me but they are thoughts of good not of evil to give me and expected in*". They forget that my ways and plans are different from theirs. And that I have the best plan for their life. Isaiah 55:8. I want what is good for them. If only my people would get out of my way, then the manifestation of my blessing would hit them and their cups would be running over. My favor and grace will overflow for them in all they do. When my people are in my way then their blessings are blocked. But out of grace I still work with them. Brenda, what do you think would happen in a person's life if they gave me full control? Ephesians 3:28 explains what would happen to them. "*I would do exceedingly, abundantly, and above all they can expect and hope for.*"** This is what the Father said to me. What a powerful revelation. **Most of the time we think we are standing in faith; but we are blocking Gods full blessing in our lives.** After the Holy Spirit gave me this revelation, I asked him when he made the statement "their cups will be running over", why do cups have a (s) on it? **God said, "Brenda you have more than one cup. You have more than one blessing that you want me to do for you. If you would get out the way then I can pour**

a blessing in every area of your life. Not only will we receive healing, we will get a financial blessing, divine protection, everything that is lacking".

God will take care of it. You will be well pleased and the joy of the Lord will be on you in all things. Now, it is seven hours later and Robert is in recovery. One of the physicians gave me an update that all went well in the surgery and that he would recover. I asked her why the surgery took so long? She responded, "Mr. Oglesby told us that he just started to hurt about three weeks ago". I confirmed that fact. She said, "When we observed his back it looked like he had been in severe pain for years". I replied that he has not been in pain. It recently started when he was not able to walk about three weeks ago. "But, it appeared to the doctors that those complications had been there for years. This takes me back to what I said earlier, Robert never received a healing. We would pray and others would pray for him but only the pain was removed. **He never became completely healed because God's plan was not to perform a miraculous healing, but God was planning to heal Robert through medicine.** You can always have faith. You can always believe God for a miracle. But, always ask God what his plans are for your life. Ask God how he wants to send the blessing. And then expect God to do what He promises. The surgery took longer than expected because of the amount of repair they had to do on his back. God had told me earlier that Robert would come out of this surgery leaping and jumping. One thing we knew and that is that he wouldn't be in pain anymore. God did perform a miracle through the physicians. Robert could have been healed long ago if we had only listened and asked God. We can save ourselves from a lot of misery if we would only let God have his way. God's way is always the right way. Today, decide to let God be God and I will do the same.

CHAPTER NINETEEN

What Comes Before Your Big Day

Are you Ready to Receive the Blessing?

God has revealed to me five things that will happen before your Big Day of Blessing. I have listed them and will discuss them in detail so that you might become aware of the things that you will have to go through and how you can survive all the circumstances.

First, God said, "that he does not send the blessing in the order that you pray".

Secondly, God said, "that I will not come when you want me to come, but I will not be late".

Thirdly, God said, "I will not deliver the blessing the way you expect but it will better than you expect".

Fourth, God said, "that you must forgive unconditionally".

And lastly, God said, "whether there will be good or bad distraction, but they will work out for your good".

First, you have to know that God does not deliver your blessing in the order that you pray for them. We have prayed for years, and some of the prayers, we have forgotten that we've ever prayed for them. But the good news is that God has not forgotten what you've asked for and as you look back at the prayers you have prayed, you will see that

God did answer this and that prayer. But most of the time God has not answered the one you were particularly looking for. The reason is that God does not answer our prayers in the order we pray them. Let me give you an example. My husband, Robert, has been praying for healing in his knees, his wrists and for his high blood pressure. He has been praying about twelve years to be healed. As of today he has not received a healing in those areas. In 2004 Robert hurt his back and the doctors told him that he would have to undergo back surgery and we added this new healing to the prayer list. In October 2004, God miraculously healed Robert's back we thought. I talk about this in my book entitled "Healing is for You". Robert received a **partial healing** from the Father. God fulfilled part of our prayer for healing, but not all of the prayer. God will fulfill all of his word in his season and in the order that he chooses. None of us have received the entire plan of what God has for our lives. But God continues to bless us from one blessing to another and God has a plan for our lives. We have to believe and trust that God will fulfill his plan for our life in his season. This is what I am talking about; God does answer our prayers but not in the order we pray them. **In God's season, God will answer all that we pray for.** Just like God healed Robert partially God will completely heal the rest of his body in due season. Oh, Great Jehovah! He is a God of mystery. God's plan is different from our plans and He does things differently than we do. That is why we must trust him. *"Truly, O God of Israel, our Savior, you work in strange and mysterious ways" (Isaiah 45:15, NLT).*

God has a divine plan and He is following his divine will for our lives. God's mission is to get his will done in the earth. God just doesn't want to bless you; his mission is to bless everyone. When you pray, most of the time, what you ask God for is only a blessing for you. **God has a bigger picture and a better plan.** Stay in God's plan; his divine will for your life so that you will get the fullness of blessing that the Father has for you. *"We have all benefited from the rich blessing he brought us one gracious blessing after another" (John 1:16, NLT).* The Message Bible states it like this, *"We all live off his generous* *bounty, gift after gift after gift"* (John 1:16, *The Message Bible*). We will receive the fullness of God's blessing in time just as the scripture says gift after gift after gift.

Secondly, God doesn't come when we want him to come, but He is right on time, and God knows what time is right for you. You don't know. God is never late. He shows up even when we think He is not there. But He is there. Stop thinking that if God doesn't show up and deliver me; then this will happen. That is not true because God does show up and those things that we think will happen to us don't even manifest. All the bad things we think that will happen to us don't even happen. We get manifest up and become disturbed about situations that hadn't happened yet and won't happen. **Trust God and He will show up. Just like God has a plan He also has a set date for your blessing.** You have to trust and wait on Him. He will answer his divine will for your life in His set time. So don't get angry, discouraged or impatient. God is always on time. And the word says, *"the Lord will send rain at the proper time from his rich treasury in heaven to bless all the work you do"* (Deuteronomy 28:12, *NLT*). At the right time and the right season God will bless you and it won't be a moment late.

Thirdly, God doesn't send the answer the way you think He should answer. God never sends us the answer the way we expect it would come. **The blessing often comes in a way we don't recognize as the blessing.** We don't even recognize that it's the answer to our long awaited prayers. But eventually, God does open our eyes to see that He has already answered our prayers and that He has answered them correctly. **What God has done and what he will do is far better than we could ever think.** When I was praying for my son, I did not recognize the answer from God when it came. Emotionally, it did not feel right, when I looked at it, it did not look right, and overall, I did not like the answer. But that answer was the best thing that has happened for my family. **We must learn how to be patient and know that God knows what he is doing and his answer is the best solution for our problems.** God is the best thing that happens to us and He has the best answer for us. We have to trust that He is working everything out on our behalf and that He has not left anything undone. *"Now to Him Who, by (in consequence of) the [action of His] power that is at work within us, is able to [carry our His purpose and] do superabundantly, far over and above all that we [dare] ask or think- infinitely beyond our highest prayers, desires, thoughts, hopes or dreams"(Ephesians 3:20, Amplified).* Hallelujah, God is able to do more than we ask or even can imagine in our small minds and small thinking. His thoughts and ways are better than ours. What we think is the best, He **can** and **will** do it better. That is why we trust and expect God to give us the most awesome blessing in all circumstances. So, when the answers to your prayers don't come the way you expect, it just might be your answer. Ask God for an open mind and heart so that you can always receive his very best for your life.

Fourthly, you must forgive before you can receive. God has called us to be forgiving people. No matter what a person or situation has done to you over the years, you must forgive. **God's logic in this is that God has forgiven you.** We have done worse things to God than people have done to us. Therefore, we must forgive our brother. Without forgiveness there will be no blessing. *"Listen to me! You can pray for anything and if you believe you will have it. But, when you are praying, first forgive anyone you are holding a grudge against, so that your Father in heaven will forgive your sins too"* (Mark 11:24-25, NLT). **God says that one of the requirements to receive your blessing is forgiveness.** We must forgive our brother unconditionally so that we can receive the fullness of God's blessings for our lives. Ask the Holy Spirit to reveal all unforgiveness in your heart, and then ask him to help you forgive. You will need God's help because this is a task that you cannot do on your own. People have been offended for years and you should not be one of them.

And lastly, there will be distractions. These distractions can be good or bad; large or small. **These distractions could be the answer to your prayers or just a distraction.** In the end if you stay in faith and trust God it will turn into something good. **Whatever**

the distraction may be, all things will work out just like God has planned. A distraction is not a trial, but a distraction is confusion about what God wants for your life. If you are not careful you will take these distractions as punishment or discipline from God and turn them into a trial. These distractions can come from God or Satan. They are a testing period. **God wants to know if we are focused on Him and his kingdom, or are we focused on what is important to us?** Are you ready to move ahead with what God wants you to do? Do you have your eyes on Jesus? We must keep our eyes on Jesus; not our problems or distractions. Distraction will stop you in your tracks; because, it takes your eyes off God and makes you focus on yourself and your accomplishments in the form of pride. **God is not trying to hurt you, but bless you.** God just wants to know if you are committed to Him and He wants you to do the best work for his kingdom. On the other hand, **when Satan is allowed by God to send you a distraction he is trying to destroy you through your commitment for God; your passion for him, and your divine covenant with God.** If Satan is successful, this will make you serve God by just going through the motions instead of serving God in love and full commitment to His kingdom. With this in mind, you need to trust God. When God sends a distraction it will turn into a blessing for us. **As we continue to believe and push forward in God then we will receive the inheritance that he has for us.** God doesn't want to send distractions to confuse us, but sometimes, it is necessary. **He would rather get our attention in love;** but, that is not always possible. So whatever means God uses to get your attention just remember it will turn out to be a blessing for you.

This is the same with Satan. God will take what He allows Satan to do and work it out so that every situation becomes a blessing to you. *"And we know that God causes everything to work together for the good of those who love God and are called according to his purpose for them"* *(Romans 8:28, NLT)*. Remember all things will work out if you keep your eyes on Jesus and the goal that God has set for you. Distractions will come before your big day of blessing to get you confused on what God is getting ready to do in your life. **But we must be like Paul, staying focused and keeping our eyes on God and the goals that He has given us, so that we might receive the victory in all things. Then we can move into our blessing in spite of the Adversity we might have endured. Amen**

REFERENCE

Life Application Study Bible, New Living Translation: Tyndale House Publishers. Wheaton, Illinois July 1996

Holy Bible, New Living Translation: Tyndale House Publishers, Inc. Wheaton, Illinois, 2004

The Master's Healing Presence Bible, King James Version: Thomas Nelson Bibles. 2003

The Amplified Old & New Testament, The Amplified Bible: Zondervan Publishing House. 1964

Webster's New World, College Dictionary: Simon & Schuster, Inc. 1997

Printed in the United States
By Bookmasters